INITIATE

AN OXFORD ANTHOLOGY OF NEW WRITING

With a Foreword by
Professor Jon Stallworthy

Edited by
Clare Morgan
Rita Ricketts

Editorial Panel
Jane Draycott
Frank Egerton
Jonathan Evans

First Published in the United Kingdom in 2010
by The Kellogg College Centre for Creative Writing

Copyright © The Kellogg College Centre for Creative Writing 2010

Copyright of Individual work remains with each author.
The moral right of the authors has been asserted.
Full details of copyright holders can be found on page 312.

A CIP catalogue record of this book
is available from the British Library

ISBN 13: 978-0-956-47760-6

Typeset in the UK by B H Blackwell Ltd, Oxford

The Kellogg College
Centre for Creative Writing
62 Banbury Road
Oxford
OX2 6PN

www.kellogg.ox.ac.uk

INITIATE

AN OXFORD ANTHOLOGY OF NEW WRITING

The Kellogg College Centre for Creative Writing

Dedicated to Corinna Wiltshire (Blackwell) who first assembled the Archive, without which the Blackwell tradition of supporting new writing would not have become widely known.

Contents

INITIATE

AN OXFORD ANTHOLOGY OF NEW WRITING

Foreword

Jon Stallworthy

Growing up in Oxford, seventy years ago, I was initiated into the mysteries of poetry and, ten years later, into those of Basil Blackwell's 'booky house' – a natural progression in his city. I remember being impressed that books bought in that shop came with a bookmark printed with lines by John Masefield, an *Oxford* poet, the Poet Laureate, no less:

> I seek few treasures, except books, the tools
> Of those celestial souls the world calls fools.
> Happy the morning giving time to stop
> An hour at once in Basil Blackwell's shop
> There, in the Broad, within whose booky house
> Half England's scholars nibble books or browse.
>
> Where'er they wander blessed fortune theirs,
> Books to the ceiling, other books upstairs:
> Books, doubtless, in the cellar, and behind
> Romantic bays, where iron ladders wind.
> And in odd nooks sometimes in little shelves,
> Lintot's and Tonson's calf-bound dainty twelves.

When, after school in a less literary city and National Service in Nigeria, I returned to Oxford as an undergraduate, my parents opened an account for me at Blackwell's, and kindly 'primed' it (with £10 or was it £20) to help me buy textbooks. These I kept to a minimum, spending the balance exclusively on poetry. W.H. Auden was then the Professor of Poetry, and I was delighted to discover a cheap copy of *Oxford Poetry 1926* that he had co-edited as an undergraduate. This introduced me to a notable series, published by Blackwells for thirty years, that alerted me to the fact that BB and Family not only offered good grazing – like no other Oxford institution – for the wo/man in the street as well as the scholar, but cared for poetry as much as profit, the new as much as the old.

I have a copy of *Oxford Poetry 1915* on my desk now. It includes undergraduate poems by Naomi Haldane (soon to be Mitchison), Aldous Huxley, Dorothy L. Sayers, and J.R.R. Tolkien; a quartet later to be celebrated for their prose rather than their poetry. Had I bought BB's *Oxford Poetry 1915* for its published price of a few shillings, I would have a work of literary history now worth something between £250 and £400.

Other Blackwell volumes of Oxford writing have also become collectors' items. *Oxford Outlook*, an anthology of poetry and prose, is perhaps the nearest to this newest venture – *Initiate* – the typescript of which is also on my desk at the moment. My feelings (so far as I can disentangle them) are gratification at being invited to launch a vessel with such an exciting crew, some of them master mariners already, others surely to become so; avid curiosity as to where they are heading and what cargo they will bring us; admiration for the builders and welders of the literary community here united; and last but not least, gratitude to the House of Blackwell – in this case in partnership with the Kellogg College Centre for Creative Writing – for continuing to sponsor a slipway for new writing from Oxford.

Recognizing the reality of *Oxford Poetry 1915* – that it featured *writers* rather than simply *poets* from an undergraduate university – and the success of Blackwell's more recent World Writers' public readings, the shipwright has commissioned a new style of vessel representative of a new-style university: one that offers, among a greatly expanded range of graduate courses, a Master of Studies in creative writing to the poets, playwrights, and novelists of tomorrow. Oxford initiates have long been more fortunate than most in working within walking distance of one of the world's greatest libraries, the Bodleian, and one of its greatest bookshops. They are now doubly fortunate in their access to the many distinguished visiting writers drawn to speak in Blackwells, at Kellogg College, and on the Masters course. They are triply fortunate in Blackwells having commissioned, in partnership with Kellogg, an anthology that brings together these rich writerly strands.

If the twentieth-century Blackwell volumes, *Oxford Poetry*, *Initiates*, *Wheels*, *Adventurers All*, and *Oxford Outlook*, can be regarded as Thames river cruisers, *Initiate* is a twenty-first-century container-ship bound for international waters. Whereas the river cruisers had mainly

British crews (the one exception in 1915 being Hasan Shahid Suhrawardy, later to become Pakistan's Ambassador to Spain), the container-ship has a truly international crew, their voices as richly varied as the genres of their cargo. I am confident this cargo will intrigue, surprise, reward all who invest in *Initiate* today and, if *Oxford Poetry 1915* offers a 600% return on investment in 2010, what profit will *Initiate* return its investors, or their descendants, in the twenty-second century?

Jon Stallworthy
Wolfson College
June 2010

Introduction

Clare Morgan

The launch of Oxford University's Master of Studies in Creative Writing in October 2005 attracted media attention and raised questions (and a few eyebrows) about the role and status of 'creative writing' in the academy. Was the awarding of a degree in creative writing appropriate to an institution such as Oxford? Would the quality of applicants stand comparison with those admitted to study for more traditional degrees? How would such an offering fare in relation to the established and high-reputation creative writing courses already provided by institutions such as the University of East Anglia or Columbia or Stanford? And what, in the end, might such a degree equip its graduates *for* – in the focused and competitive market places of the twenty-first century, what might Oxford's MSt in Creative Writing provide?

From the outset it was clear that there would be no shortage of applicants, and there have consistently been more than ten for every place on offer. The breadth of our application field represents the wealth of creative talent present in the global community. This is particularly important to us, as one of the central principles around which the course has been built is the value of cross-cultural interchange for creative writing. Our current cohort includes students from Cyprus, Singapore, Canada, Australia, Sweden, Denmark, Ireland, and the USA, as well as UK students from a wide range of backgrounds. Next year we will be welcoming, among our intake, a Rhodes Scholar from Kenya and fiction writer from Nepal.

The breadth of talent and potential among our graduates is demonstrated in this first 'showcase anthology' of their writing – *Initiate*. In its pages, writers from our first three graduating years are represented. Our fiction writers, poets, and dramatists are offering you, the reader, a snapshot of what they have been producing. These are punctuation points in the long process of writerly development that is the lot of all who choose to pursue writing as a career. Some, inevitably (and however

9

talented they may be) will turn away from writing to pursue some other, more immediately visible or materially rewarding occupation. Others, perhaps in these pages still quietly developing their skills, will rise, through dedication, luck and that nugget of intense individuality that we call 'voice', to achieve success through having their fiction or their poetry or their drama taken up and out to a wider audience. Then they will know the thrill of speaking not to a few, but to many. And then they will know, gradually and cumulatively, the further demands that writing will make on them if they choose to place it as the hard task-master at the very centre of their lives.

The writers represented in these pages are not only graduates of Oxford's MSt in Creative Writing – the 'initiates' in this endlessly fascinating, endlessly demanding process. These pages also feature those who have facilitated the process of initiation. Not, in this first anthology, the dedicated team of tutors – published writers themselves – who have worked with our students and nurtured them on these early and highly developmental steps of their writerly journey; nor those among their number who have given their time and expertise as members of the Editorial Panel, and without whose invaluable contribution this publication would not have come about. It will fall to the successor-publications of *Initiate* to display the great range of talent present among the members of our tutor team.

In this first publication we are celebrating some of the many writers from around the world who have worked with our students as visiting readers, speakers or supporters – who have so generously brought to Oxford's MSt in Creative Writing their voices, their beliefs, their writing, and themselves. Our visiting readers, speakers and supporters, some home-grown Oxford writers, some from other parts of the UK, others from as far afield as Guyana or the Indian subcontinent, have enriched enormously the writerly understandings that our students have acquired during their time with us. Both in the fabric of our course-offering and in their participation in readings showcasing our students in the Blackwell World Writers in Oxford series, they have helped our graduates towards modes of expression suited for the conditions of our complex and swiftly-changing world.

It will be for others to judge which of our graduate writers may in the future be taken up and out to a wider audience. Many are already achieving publication successes, and the breadth of the cross-genre opportunities offered on the course has enabled a number of them to become successful in modes of writing with which they were unfamiliar when they first joined us. They are also achieving success in the professions, being appointed to teaching posts in literature and creative writing in other universities.

A central belief of the Oxford course, and one which I relished incorporating into its design, is that good readers make good writers. Or to put it another way, it is very difficult to achieve one's potential as a writer unless one's reading skills have been honed and developed in a consistent and purposeful way. This belief has motivated the happy collaboration of Blackwell with the Kellogg College Centre for Creative Writing in publishing this anthology. I am particularly grateful to Andrew Hutchings, C.E.O of Blackwell, and to Gareth Hardy and the Blackwell team, for their dedication in bringing this publication to fruition.

An emphasis on the vital relationship between reading and writing, combined with the range of voices and approaches we bring to the Oxford course, benefits greatly, I believe, the development of that individual voice which is at the heart of all compelling prose, poetry and drama. I hope that readers of this first anthology will enjoy their encounter with the range of voices on offer in these pages – the initiates and those who have contributed to the process of initiation – on which the richness and variety of our literary heritage depends.

Clare Morgan
Kellogg College, Oxford
July 2010

Prompted to Adventure

A Blackwell Legacy

Rita Ricketts

*'The constant discovery of the unknown, the encouragement
of talent, or even the finding of genius; the excitement of the
calculated risk and the vindication of judgement'.*

The publication of this new anthology, *Initiate*, which assumed its own
identity from the first, springs from an Oxford tradition that dates at
least from early medieval times and a Blackwell tradition going back
more than a century. Just as timeless is the problem of getting published.
Here was a huge black hole into which most writers fell! The early
Blackwells, Benjamin Harris (1813-1855) and Benjamin Henry (BHB:
1849-1924), would-be writers themselves, understood only too well what
it felt like to be in this cavernous gap. Benjamin Harris died early and
it was left to his son to close it, setting-up his own publishing house,
B H Blackwell, in 1879. BHB resolved to remove from new writers 'the
reproach of insolvency', and he thought nothing of working into the
early hours to correct their proofs at no cost to themselves. Neither
born of a love of money nor of a desire to achieve worldly success, this
assistance in bringing forth the offspring of writers 'unknown to fame'
provided scant dividend until the late 1920s.

BHB, forced to leave school at the age of thirteen, honed his writing and
editing skills by studying Quaritch's famous catalogues and producing
his own, during a bookselling apprenticeship as lengthy as Jacob's was
to Laban. Teaching himself Latin, Greek and poetry when customers
were scarce, he tested his memory on early morning runs around Christ
Church Meadow, *brushing with eager steps the dew away*. It was this
intense interest in poetry, and BHB's knowledge and sympathetic ear,
which attracted writers to his bookshop. Of these, Balliol's 'nest of
singing birds' caught his attention; just as those of Oxford University's

Master of Studies in Creative Writing have caught the ear of Blackwell today. In the book shop's first year, the imprint B H Blackwell made its debut with a slender brochure entitled *Mensae Secundae: Verses Written in Balliol*. Its successful reception led to *Primavera* and *Waifs and Strays*, which together with *Oxford Verses*, foreshadowed the first Blackwell *Oxford Poetry* (1910) and many individual collections. The American poet Christopher Morley recalled Mr Blackwell's 'little booklets bound in paper and sold (if at all) for a shilling each'; such volumes as *Ignes Fatui* and *Metri Gratia* by Philip Guedalla of Balliol and *Play Hours with Pegasus* by A P Herbert of New College.

Preoccupied with the bookshop, BHB bequeathed his infant publishing house to his son, Basil Blackwell (BB: 1989-1994). And despite Robert Bridges' warning not to enter the 'perilous seas' of publishing, it burgeoned. BB's 1914 selection for *Oxford Poetry*, introduced by Gilbert Murray and edited by G D H Cole, Geoffrey Denis and Sherard Vines, contained early work by Philip Guedalla, Michael Sadler and A P Herbert. Close on their heels, between 1916-1952, came contributions from J R R Tolkien, Aldous Huxley, Dorothy L. Sayers, Siegfried Sassoon, Vera Brittain, Edmund Blunden, Robert Graves, Robert Graves, Graham Greene, Cecil Day-Lewis, Auden, Louis MacNeice, Stephen Spender, Philip Larkin, Roy Porter, Kingsley Amis, Elizabeth Jennings and Oxford's now Professor of Poetry Geoffrey Hill; more recent 'names' include Fleur Adcock, David Constantine, Carol Ann Duffy, John Fuller, Seamus Heaney, W.N. Herbert, Elizabeth Jennings, Andrew Motion, Paul Muldoon, Bernard O'Donoghue, Tom Paulin, Mario Petrucci, Craig Raine and many more.

Blackwell's *Adventurers All*, 'a series of young poets unknown to fame', complemented *Oxford Poetry*: introducing newcomers such as Claude Collier Abbot and the 'Georgian-toned' Richard Church. Wilfred Owen's work was published posthumously in *Wheels* (1919); also including that of the Sitwells and Aldous Huxley. In addition, some writers saw their own collections emerge from the Blackwell stable. Harold Acton's, for example, was the envy of undergraduates when they saw the multi-coloured binding of his first book of poems, *Aquarium*, in Blackwell's shop. This present anthology's near namesake, *Initiates*, was described as 'a series of poetry by approved hands in uniform volumes, set in dolphin old style type ... on boards at three shillings net'. The first, *In the Valley of Vision* was by Geoffrey Faber followed by Eleanor Farjeon's *Sonnets and Poems*, Aldous Huxley's *The Defeat of*

Youth, and other Poems, *Songs for Sale: an anthology of verse* edited by E B C Jones and Edith Sitwell's *Clowns' Houses*.

As a series that included a variety of new writing, it is Blackwell's *Oxford Outlook* that provides the nearest model for this present anthology. It included poetry, prose and polemic that sometimes sailed close to the wind in Edwardian England. The roll call of English writers, cutting their teeth there, is impressive. John Betjeman made an early debut, 'never having come out as an Oxford Poetry poet', as a joint editor with John Sparrow. The first volume of *Oxford Outlook* (1919) included the work of John Masefield, A E Shipley (Vice-Chancellor of Cambridge) and Siegfried Sassoon. The second added Gilbert Murray, Beverley Nichols, Dorothy L Sayers and Vera Brittain (both arguing for co-education: that women, many of whom had returned from 'war-work', should be awarded degrees). Subsequent volumes were edited by Julian Huxley, Harold Acton, C Day Lewis and W H Auden, Louis McNeice, Isaiah Berlin, A L Rouse, Douglas Jay and Richard Goodman, Emlyn Williams and Patrick Monkhouse. L P Hartley, Christopher Isherwood, Emlyn Williams, D H Lawrence, Edouard Roditi, William Empson, Douglas Jay, Maurice Bowra, Gilbert Highet, Eric Gill, J Middleton Murray and Myfanwy Evans. Basil Blackwell remembered that Stephen Spender, who had edited the 1929 volume, had from the start 'intimations of immortality'.

But Blackwell's literary activities were not restricted to publishing. They were also anxious that new writers should be heard, in public. BHB's earliest venture was undertaken in co-operation with Balliol. Styled as The Horace Club, Benjamin Henry acted as entrepot and keeper of the records. Their tongues loosened by wine, 'each [poet] was bound to produce and read to his fellows, a poem written for the occasion 'in a well-known language' and not exceeding in length, not falling below in brevity, any poem of Horace (excluding the *De Arte Poetica*)'. Members included Asquith, Belloc and John Buchan, A D Godley, St. John Lucas, Arnold Ward (great nephew of Matthew Arnold), H C Beeching, Laurence Binyon, A E Zimmern, Meade Falkner and W R Hardy (who invariably produced a poem in Greek). Benjamin Henry, in his meticulous way, had kept an autographed copy of the poems, pasting them into an album at the end of each meeting. These records were subsequently published, serving as 'a moving monument to Victorian wit and scholarship'.

A decade later BB and his sister Dorothy held a series of Saturday evening readings. And Vera Brittain turned to them for her muses and for solace. In the autumn of 1919, she wrote to her mother that she had been invited by Basil and Dorothy Blackwell 'to a social circle of more or less literary people ... every Saturday evening and which I feel inclined to join'. She, like Dorothy L Sayers, had her reward: publication. In the summer of 1920 Basil invited Vera to edit the next Volume of *Oxford Poetry*, which incorporated her poem 'The Lament of the Demobilised' – one that resonates today. It was in this spirit, while writing my history of Blackwellians, that I set up the *World Writers at Blackwell* readings and On the Fringe at Blackwell for the Sunday Times Oxford Literary Festival. Since the readings have been re-introduced several new writers have gone on to earn their 'Blues', but I wanted more to share their luck. To this end I joined forces with Clare Morgan, Director of the Kellogg College Centre for Creative Writing and founder of Oxford's Master of Studies in Creative Writing, with a view to securing publication of their work. Blackwell enthusiastically agreed to produce, jointly with Kellogg College, an anthology showcasing the best new writing of M.St. Students who had come to Oxford from around the world.

The American poet Christopher Morley described his attempts to get published in 1921. 'What I remember best of my bashful interview with Mr Blackwell senior', Morley wrote, 'besides his pink face and white hair and extreme politeness, was his asking me to put in some more commas.' He told Morley that he liked his poems but 'there don't seem to be any commas in them. Perhaps you don't use commas much in America?' Mr Blackwell's bark was worse than his bite, and duly Morley's poems came out, with or without 'proper' punctuation. True to earlier Blackwell tradition, contributors to this anthology are also drawn from outside the University; nearly a century ago Edith Sitwell pleaded that Blackwell publications should not be restricted. Breaking with tradition, some contributors to this first issue of *Initiate* are already household names. But just as with early Blackwell publications, it is the relative newcomers that form the nucleus of this anthology, writing upon 'a remarkable variety of subjects'. If they, too, should also find a place on the world stage, this will be a rich reward for a simple endeavour and a fitting memorial to the pioneering work of the Blackwells.

It is appropriate that Julian Blackwell should have the last word. He is delighted that his grandfather's and father's pioneering work in publishing is not forgotten. This latest publication also demonstrates Blackwell's continuing commitment to Oxford University: its colleges and scholars, and all its writers and readers. When Edith Sitwell's *The Mother* was selling so slowly it might have had to be pulped, a Blackwell employee, S T Fenemore – himself a poet at heart – bought six copies, giving them as presents to his family and colleagues. Such is the dedication shown by Blackwellians, dating back over a century and three quarters! 'Times may have changed, but Blackwell's has not.' Reference must also be made to the directors of Wiley Blackwell, especially Philip Carpenter, who generously gifted back the file copies of Blackwell publications, and to the Bodleian and Merton College for giving them a home, where their treasures can be unearthed and preserved.

Blackwell's world famous shop in Broad Street, which opened in 1879, has almost a symbiotic relationship with the University and generations of writers have come, as Hilaire Belloc famously recorded, to 'draw their draughts from the black wells'. Sir John Betjeman had recalled the variety of all the 'beautifully printed' Blackwell volumes: 'decadent some of them, folksy and some of them obscure – passionate all of them ... put forward at the one time in our lives when we really felt we must be published'. May this Kellogg-Blackwell publication afford this new generation of writers the same inspiration, opportunity and recognition. Floreat!

Rita Ricketts
Visiting Scholar Bodleian Library
Merton College, June 2010

The Butterfly Tide

Sophy Roberts

The Butterfly Tide

Chapter One

When he pulled off his hat, he knew exactly how he must have looked to the others: like a cockatoo, his coarse blonde hair stuck up into a crest by the salt and sweat. The storm was over but his ears still rang with the noise of wind lashing against steel. The lines around his eyes stung from the spray, and his fingers — clumsy with cold — felt as if they were no longer his.

It had been a tough night for the *Aurora*. As tough as they get, thought Tómas Eyvindsson as he unpeeled his oilskins for the first time in hours. He was exhausted. He could already feel the swelling where a cable had bruised the back of his thigh. His lips were cracked so that when he spoke he could taste his own blood seeping on to his tongue.

He lit a cigarette, the rasp of the match lingering in the cold. When he coughed, the pain went out into his lungs. It made him wonder if he'd cracked a rib when he was thrown against the winch. He remembered how he had failed to turn back and throw a prayer to the statue of the Virgin standing at the harbour mouth. One of the freezer trawlers had been coming in too tight. If he'd been able, Tómas would have paused to pay his respects as he steered in close, passing the skua perched on the statue's meekly bowed head.

Tómas didn't like to lay stock by these things, but still, it bothered him when an hour into their trip they found a banana on board. It was a blackened skin in the heads, the flesh soft and sweet. *You're never too important to listen to the omens* — that's what Vagn had said. At the time Tómas shrugged it off. He'd taken it as another of Vagn's digs, the fact skippers earn more than engineers.

They hadn't expected anything unusually rough. For Southeast Iceland, the forecast had been variable four at first, and gale six to seven in the east. But out on the water it looked more ominous than that, the heave more menacing as if the storm was building up under the surface of the sea. That's when Tómas had made the men fetch their safety hats. He didn't want to be the one who got sued just because he hadn't followed the rules. It was absurd, what a skipper was liable for these days. And if the politicians got their way, it would only get worse.

At first it hadn't looked like much — a few angry squalls ripping the top off the water to create bursts of smoke. But just as the sun should have shown its face the skies had changed to a dead, resolute grey. What concerned him most, partly because he'd seen it so rarely, was the fast descending darkness when the Arctic sun normally sat low on the noon horizon before it dipped again by four.

Tómas soon had the lads draw in the nets. They secured the fish-hold just in time — that was when the loose warp had whipped him to the floor. The baiting machine was made safe, the longlines put away. But that was about all because the storm got worse quicker than Tómas had anticipated. Not much later and he was unable to draw the line between water and sky as wave upon wave, each more swollen than the next, broke broadside against the *Aurora*'s hull, the wind ripping at the wheelhouse door as if the fingers of God were trying to open up the trawler and gut her alive.

They hunkered down in the wheelhouse to ride out the brutal pitch and roll. Soon Tómas was unable to hear the radio above the pummelling of the waves. Nor could he read the radar, water thundering across the glass in eighty knot gusts. It was raining sideways. The autopilot was useless, the gale more formidable than anything his machines could manage as blips flashed and died on screens, with one — his GPS — losing power entirely.

When it got like this, it was better not to fight it; Tómas had learnt that much in the days his father had skippered the *Aurora* through these waters without all her fancy electronics. Those were the days fishermen read the stars rather than satellite constellations clustered on computers. So Tómas knew what to expect, that a good trawlerman relied on nothing except his prayers when it got this bad. You looked out for lights to avoid a collision, but otherwise you closed your eyes with every breach and tried not to lose your gear.

By the time deep night was upon them, water was coming in and more than Tómas would have liked. Vomit from all four of them covered the wheelhouse floor. The rail down to the bunks had broken off while one of the bilge pumps struggled to function in the bow. Just when he thought it couldn't get much worse, the storm tore at her again — hissing rollers Tómas couldn't help but count as he waited for the seventh wave. That's the one that's said to bear you down into unknown depths even scanners cannot sound, the one that's said to call your name as it towers overhead. *The seventh wave.* Last night Tómas had thought it was finally going to come, out here on the fringe of Iceland's fishing grounds where storms drive you out into the wide black rill that makes up the North Atlantic Drift: warm, fathomless, racing towards the ice.

'Whu's gunna make some feckin' tea.'

Pavel stood smoking on the bow. He could have passed as one of them — an Icelander, thought Tómas — his skin was so bloodless from the storm. Except for when he spoke. His accent was a mix of Scottish, from where he'd worked the fish market, and American, which he must have picked up from television.

'I said whu's gunna make some feckin' tea.'

Vagn grunted and prised off some tobacco glued to his lip. Niels said something about it being Pav's feckin' turn, feckin' was, feckin' tea was his feckin' job. Tómas watched the Pole rise to the taunt. It always happened when the boy thought they were taking the piss, which they invariably were, mocking the way he spoke, the way he nervously tugged at his ear. Trouble was the lad always let it show. *Feck you*, said the boy, kicking at a rusted rail. Vagn and Niels smiled at one another. Tómas, too tired to reason with any of them, handed the boy his mug of steaming tea laced with boiled Coca-Cola.

Nothing had been said last night when it happened. They were all four on deck trying to fix the hatch when the wind and the tide had moved apart, the trawler sinking into a wide and silent trough. The kid was new to the game; he'd worked on fruit farms near Derry and after that, taped up lobster claws beneath the Clyde to send to restaurants in Manhattan; he hadn't reckoned on the tricks the sea can play, on how it can slam you into chasms as deep as valleys and suddenly fall still. So when the trough had opened up, the boy had hoped, Tómas supposed, that the roar of wind and water would somehow conceal his fear. He'd misread the signs that Tómas had come to know so well. For sometimes, even in the depths of a storm, there can open up a hole in the sea. It is a space of perfect silence, a moment of division as if the great Atlantic has sucked in all its breath and is holding it close before unleashing the very worst of its power. Tómas had seen it before, up towards Dalvík. And so it was last night, the night of the storm. While the *Aurora* slipped into the belly of the lull, the boy, not knowing what was happening, had started calling for his mother.

A moment of division, that was all it was. And then Tómas, feeling the darkness grow above them, fell down on the boy, driving him to the floor as the two waves broke against each other and pushed the deck under the water. A few seconds later and she popped up like a cork onto the swell, their bodies pinned to the deck like a pair of drowned flies.

Tómas continued to undress. He peeled off his long johns, his skin damp and itchy. He hadn't had to do that in a while — piss in his oilskins. The smell of his own sweat wafted up towards him, mixed in with salt spray and diesel. The salt had soaked into the weave of his sweater and where it was dry, had stiffened around his neck.

The smell of my father, thought Tómas.

Maybe it was true, that no man ever left the fleet because it was a stink you could never get rid of however hard you scrubbed and polished and bleached the stench from your skin. His wife hated it, which is why she bought him some God-awful soap. *Like being flayed*, he'd tell her. *Well it's good enough for the whalers in Jap*an, she'd insist, and sure enough, she would order it on the Internet from some middleman in Anchorage. Some smart little prick more like who'd worked out how to make a buck from anxious fishermen's wives.

Lately, however, he'd noticed a more peculiar development. She'd taken to saying she could smell when a trawlerman had died from the smoke emitted by the crematorium. Fishy, she said, like herring left forgotten in the smokehouse. She said it was worse than listening to the shipping forecast — the fact she could never get away from the smell because they lived just a block from the chimney. Tómas tried to point out it's not the trawlermen who get burnt; it's the foreigners and Witnesses and the Seventh Day Adventists. How could she smell herring? When that didn't work he tried to joke her out of it. He told her the scent she described would be nothing on the blue inferno when she went up in flames. Valium burns better than meths, he told her, all the while observing how her eyes had darkened around the edges, the blue-grey smudges of exhaustion seeping into her skin.

Tómas needed to rest. He was looking forward to it. Out on a still ocean was among the few places he could sleep peacefully, his body floating above the darkness where the ocean is deeper than the sky. Fishing was in his blood. He knew it, for with his bunk gently pitching in the swell his dreams had a sharpness he could never find on land. His father used to say they were different — the dreams that belong to fishermen. He said they were God-given strategies to make the nights appear less empty. And so it was for Tómas. The dreams he had at sea helped him forget his wife and son.

That's why he didn't like the presence of the boy. The way he'd been calling for his mother during the storm brought back memories Tómas would rather have forgotten. Like when he'd watched Íris crying at the harbour, her belly swollen as if it might split open at any minute. But he left all the same, and when he returned, had a son. There were other memories, too, crowding in on him. As their boy had grown older, he'd wanted them both to stand there on the breakwater, for them to wave him off with tears in their eyes. But it never happened quite as he had hoped. Instead his wife bundled their son into the pink pushchair he had picked up at a garage sale the winter of their son's birth when he'd been fishing the Greenland Banks. He'd watched them from the bow as they waited for a bus, his wife never once looking through the rain to see the face of a man who still loved her more than she realised, even if he didn't quite know how to live happily on land, or to tell her how he missed her. And so he did what he had to do: skippered the *Aurora* safely through the weather, only occasionally broke the quotas. He worked hard, repainted her one year in four. He looked after his crew as well as any in the fleet — a reputation he was proud of — and last year even made enough money to buy a holiday in Spain.

A holiday in Spain. The notion of a golden beach had never felt more alien. The scene in front of him now, however, was as familiar as rain.

As after every big storm he'd known, the ocean was flat in the still, low-lying fog. Sometimes the sun cut through, splicing the oily-slick of water, the shaft of light forming a ribbon of mercury where it met the surface of the sea. But otherwise, neither sound nor movement broke the silence.

'It was like this when the *Bibiana* went down,' Niels said, pouring himself some coke.

The boy spat at the deck.

'Never heard of the *Bibiana*, boy? Disappeared like a leaf down a drain. One minute she was there and thwipp, she was gone. Like a leaf down a drain.'

The boy didn't answer but watched his spittle slip across the steel.

'Under us all the time. Volcanoes on the seabed throwing up their methane. I'm telling you. Melts your nets before you know it. That's what happened to the trawler, *Jóhanna* she was called, fishing the back of the Westmans the day before she blew.'

'Feckin' liar.'

'It's true. Sea was bubbling like a witch's cauldron. But it's the gas you've got to mind. We could be riding some now and before you know it, bang, the bubble pops, and thwipp, down we go, three hundred feet back into the water like a leaf down a drain. That's a big drop for any vessel. Causes it to spilt and sink in seconds.'

'Saw it, did ye'?'

'Happens when you least expect it.'

'Ye' lying shite.'

Vagn looked up from where he was mending a cable, his legs stretched out stiffly in front of him. 'Happened to the *Sefarina*,' he said in his customary drawl. 'She was fishing Satan's Hole when the same thing happened. Except up she came again. They had to take the middle out of her after that. Next time we all saw her she was twelve feet shorter. Shrunk, she was, like she'd been put through a hot wash.'

Vagn pulled off his hat and smiled slyly at Niels. The boy smiled too, although Tómas could see an uneasiness in his response, a look that reminded Tómas of the last rookie he'd taken on. Finnur, he was called, in 1994. A quiet kid from Heimaey who used to take Beta Blockers for his shakes. Depression they said when they found his skins on the fo'c'sle. Heroin, said the coroner, when his body eventually washed up on Surtsey. He'd been discovered by a scientist studying the origins of life.

BOY MISTAKEN FOR MERMAID, read the headline in Reykjavik.

'Nah, that's Finnur Amundsen,' said Tómas when later that summer, he identified the kid on the slab. It was the first dead body he'd seen, and to Tómas it looked surprisingly well preserved. Someone said that's what smack does to you — keeps you looking fresh. Tómas, however, thought it more likely to be the work of the winter ice, his flesh the same dull grey as the blocks that slip off the glaciers to clog the sea out west.

Tómas cut the engine. He asked Vagn to check it over before the next of the weather blew in. Niels and the boy he sent below deck to catch up on sleep. He'd rest later. For now Tómas sank into the plastic chair that he brought out on top. He closed his eyes but not before turning on the radio to listen to the news.

He didn't know how long he'd been sitting there, or even if he was listening to a repeat of the story he'd heard an hour before. He wouldn't have even looked up it if there hadn't been the cry of the herring gulls.

He wondered if another trawler had crept into the sweep of their radar without any of them registering. Strange, though. The fog was thick. But the screaming gulls, it was as if they were within yards of the *Aurora*. And so Tómas kept on staring. That's when he noticed the skeleton of a boat emerging out of the mist.

It was a sailing yacht, a two-masted schooner probably about twenty feet in length. The russet-coloured sails were half down, or so it appeared, the rigging knotted and torn.

'Vagn. Vagn!' Tómas shouted.

Vagn's head emerged from the engine room, his face greasy with oil. He rubbed his hands against his overalls and came towards Tómas at the same slow pace he did everything, in storm or calm.

'Do you see?'

Vagn shook his head. 'Fog's too thick.'

'The mast's broken, Vagn.'

For a couple of minutes the two men stood in silence, staring at the sea.

'I'll start her up,' Vagn said as he lit another cigarette.

They kept the *Aurora's* engine to a mutter as they curved towards the vessel. The gulls lifted, wheeling into the air. And then silence. For there was still no tremble of wind, the *Aurora* barely dimpling the greasy plain of sea.

'Don't like the smell of it,' Vagn said.

'Pull in to starboard.'

'You'll regret it.'

'Harder.'

Now they were within a few yards of her, Tómas could see she was long and slim and handsome, a boat that looked like it had been built at the turn of the last century and carrying an Irish flag. But with her broken mast she was also the most sorrowful thing he'd encountered in all his years at sea. She was longer than he'd first calculated, measuring more like thirty feet over the deck, the kind of boat that would require a crew of two or more. Her name was *Ballylin*.

'Hoy!' Tómas shouted. This caused more birds to scatter from where they'd been feeding on something in the hatch.

'Hold this,' Tómas said, handing the boy a rope as the kid emerged groggy-eyed on to the *Aurora's* deck.

'Am no' goin' near the feckin' thing.'

Tómas ignored the boy and instead tied the rope to the trawler himself. He gave a frustrated shake of his head as he pulled himself over the side of the *Aurora* and hung off the ladder. He slung the rope on to the yacht and strained to loop it under the bow rail, pulling gently until the two vessels kissed each other's sides.

He picked his way carefully across the deck laid with lengths of solid teak, steadying himself with the boom as he stepped over canvas. She was a well-loved boat, that much he could tell from the deep patina of the deck and the way the planks had been caulked with cotton, the wooden cleats and polished brass finishes. But her masts and spars, they were too fragile to be out here drifting like the spores of dandelions across the ocean. It moved him more than he expected, the thought of the boat in the storm, her narrow frame thrown about until her sails were stretched to breaking, taut and thin as skin pulled over a collarbone. He thought of the effort it must have taken to pull in the canvas, of the rip of the jib and the crew being thrown off from the bowsprit, their bodies bobbing briefly until swamped by another roller. Left on her own, a yacht this slender wouldn't have been able to protect herself. She seemed too petite, too elegant to take on the weather and the winter.

Suddenly the yacht's radio cut in — the crackle of co-ordinates, the name of a winter cruise ship. Then the voices disappeared. Identifying where the noise had come from, Tómas proceeded through the hatch in the foredeck and down into the galley.

*

Later, much later, when his wife asked him how it happened, he'd say he didn't know why he didn't stop to consider what he might discover when he stepped inside. He just did it, as if what lay concealed within the schooner had already exerted its power, drawing him into its world of secrets and loss. Like finding a message in a bottle that was never intended to be read, that's what he told her: the discovery of this tragedy that should never have occurred.

But he didn't give her any more detail. There wasn't any need, for had he described what he'd really seen, Tómas Eyvindsson knew his wife would have never slept again.

The man was lying at the foot of the stairs staring at nothing, his hair plastered down onto his scalp. His eyes were showing just their whites under his half-closed lids. They were puffed up and creamy like those of a fish poached in brine. Water a couple of inches deep had got in under the door. He must have been forty years old, and tall, a good six feet or more. He was dark — even in the wet Tómas could see a curl to his hair — and clean-shaven. He had a strong jaw, an elegant nose that fell steeply from his forehead, and wide, high cheekbones. Where light caught it around the temples, his hair was peppered grey. He was surrounded by a sodden wool blanket, a buff colour that smelt from the wet. His leg was thrust out at an awkward angle, it was clearly broken, and his head was cradled in a milky pool formed by a burst carton of UHT.

Tómas pulled his turtleneck up over his mouth. He didn't retch, he didn't even pull back for a clean breath, but stepped over the body and pulled himself on to a banquette so he could better survey what lay before him.

He noticed the texture of the seat, the feel of the soft cream leather and beeswaxed table. Nice, he thought, as fancy as he'd come across. On the floating milk carton he could read an English label. There was a use-by date of 13 March 2009 — another three months away. Parts of a fly-tying kit had been scattered about the floor. There were feathers, hooks, strips of metallic blue and gold floating on the water. And on the wall was an icon, or at least that's what it looked like to Tómas, depicting a saint's head circled in gold. There were books, too, hardbacks on Irish gardens, salmon fishing as well as a row of a dozen or so antique volumes. He opened one up. It was written in English and featured botanical drawings.

I need to find the log-book, thought Tómas, need to check if there's any more crew to account for. So he began moving through the length of the boat, running his finger along a groove in the rosewood panelling. But there was nothing out of place. Just neatly made beds, teabags thrown about the sink and a half-eaten tin of tuna that smelt as if it had been left a day in the sun. The gimballed cooker hung motionless, the needle on the steering compass not even shivering. It was dumfounding. It looked as if there was no-one else on board and that there never had been in the first place, as if this man lying at the bottom of the stairs had taken the yacht out alone with barely a change of clothes.

And then some old photographs clipped to florescent fishing line and strung above the berth to the stern. Tómas twisted them towards the light coming through a side-port. One of the images depicted a large house surrounded by lawn, another a vast greenhouse sharply drawn against the sky — it looked as if it were positioned on a cliff-edge — flanked by tall trees. There was one of the yacht cutting through tropical waters, and then another picture, this in black and white, of a Cornish Crabber pulled up alongside a slipway covered in seaweed and mussels. The largest picture, which Tómas unclipped, showed a woman laughing at the camera. She was maybe thirty, forty years of age, with long dark hair and narrow wrists. Her trousers were rolled up as she stood in deserted shallows, a wave breaking against her shins. To one side of her, the colours bleached out, the film overexposed, stood a boy of about four. He was wearing a short-sleeved wetsuit, squinting up into the sky.

'He's dead,' Tómas shouted.

'Feckin' knew it,' Pavel said, shaking his head.

'Mary Mother of Christ' Niels said. He had joined the others on the deck of the trawler.

'You'd think it happened last night but I'm not so sure. I don't think we could move him.'

'Feckin' right we dinne feckin' move him.'

'Any more of them?'

Tómas shook his head. He stepped back into the cabin. He was right; there was no way they could shift him. His distended stomach meant his body would probably puncture with the stress. They'd tow in the yacht, that's what they'd do, until the Coast Guard could reach them. Towards the coast the forecast was still mixed so chances were the helicopters would be grounded for another day. Besides, with the man dead, his rescue would hardly be prioritised. Tómas tried to think it through sensibly. Unless they were already on another job in close waters, the patrol vessel would come from Faxagarður. Never near when you need them, thought Tómas, remembering an incident the previous autumn. The bastards had run a spot check out on the water. It took a full four hours of fingering every pollock in his catch in the hope they might find something illegal. Some dodgy meshing, perhaps, or an out-of-date licence.

Tómas drew out of his pocket the photograph he'd unclipped of the woman and child and made his decision. He'd do what was right. There was the threat of fouling his propeller by towing in the yacht. And they'd lose a week's fishing, which wasn't great. But that's just the way it would have to be, thought Tómas, all the while remembering the eyes on the poor bastard and how his body's juices were already leaking into the bilges. Because that's was what it all came to in the end — just another man dead on the water leaving a family to make sense of it. He knew he'd have hell to pay the crew, what with coming back with only a handful of saithe from a few hours of fishing. But you've got to respect the sea, Tómas told himself, got to heed the unspoken rules or it will swallow you up and pin you to the seabed along with everyone else who thought they were bigger than the ocean.

Tómas crossed himself and turned to leave. He wasn't a religious man, but it somehow felt the right thing to do. And that's when he caught his leg on a metal box wedged beneath the stairs. On it were painted the letters J. M. Hathaway, County Kerry.

Tómas heaved it out of the cabin under his arm. Again, he didn't think about what it might contain but instead opened it up on deck to reveal a pile of handwritten pages, of neatly folded boat plans and charts. He pulled out a passport, a British passport, and a score of dead and broken butterflies fell from between the pages.

'We've found our man,' he shouted, mesmerised by the tiny wings running through his fingers.

*

Tómas was in his bunk. It had taken more than an hour to secure the yacht to the *Aurora*. He knew he needed to sleep more than ever, but the discovery was irresistible. The silky touch of the butterflies, the dust from their wings staining his fingertips that were as rough as a cow's tongue.

The A4 papers had been carefully organised, tied together with one of those green treasury tags his wife used for his accounts. There were just a few pencil scrawls crossing out sentences, sometimes whole pages, but most of it was legible. Among the bound sheets — Tómas reckoned on a couple of hundred or so — were images of moths the colours of ploughed fields. There were some loose printed emails with invoices made out in euros, 3,000, 7,000, 300 apiece. There were also pages torn from a book. These paragraphs of text had been deliberately stapled to the handwritten notes, some words circled, others with arrows pointing towards neat amends in red.

There were also a few loose salmon flies, Tómas recognised a Thunder and Lightning, and another passport, a newer passport, its green covers barely soiled. The photograph was of the same child in the wetsuit. Connor Hathaway. Place of Birth: Cobh, Ireland. 09 APR/AVR 04.

Later that evening Tómas could hear the crew talking on deck.

'I did'ne' sign up to this shite. Draggin' a dead man in behind us with another front comin' in with the speed of a feckin' Jap's train.'

'Skipper's right, though, we can't pretend we didn't see him.'

'He probably just fell over in the storm.'

'Wha' the feck is a boat like that doin' up here in January anyway?'

'The boy's right. And no word of her on the open channel.'

'Come on, man, which of us were listening?'

'Doesn't add up, that's all I'm saying.'

Tómas listened to the conversation trail off. He would deal with the boy later, tell him how things worked and what it meant to leave a dead man floating. Bad luck, it was; couldn't get much badder. Worse than a stray banana, that's what he'd tell him. For now, however, Tómas Eyvindsson lay back in his bunk and began to read.

Poems

David Krump

An Ample Tree

In preparation for his simple death
my brother gathers his uniforms, dried boots,
a collectible bible and apples fallen
from an ample tree. These he places
into a discarded oak barrel he's pulled
from the slough. The oak staves have swollen
tight. He drops the apples in last and asks
that I keep the barrel, a gift. *No, right*
beside the table-vice, he advises
when I make to roll it to the corner,
empty but for the shed push-broom's bristles.
In garage light, he twitches, hands over
his revolver, two dense pounds heavier
than it looks, little thing. How mistaken my offer
to store this barrel must seem to him. I'm often
mistaken—not an ample tree, but a maple tree
drops these oddest apples, accolades of the fall.

Ownership

I haven't started my car in ten days.
It's gathering parking tickets under
its stiff wiper. On its roof snow lofts
as high and soft as Russian diplomat's winter hat.

It's weeks of this until the cop stops
digging for the wiper beneath heavy snow.
An orange tow-notice he sticks – no, he slaps –
to the driver's side window. He shows
his humanity like an amateur ghost.

In five days, he'll know what I know.
My car will start just fine and the only
working tow-truck in this town is mine.
We own what we own. He will phone me
for assistance again. *There's this stubborn brown
car. Check your messages. I need help.*

I will win. I will not kill myself.

The Evening We Hang Bad Joe

Only a small crowd forms. Sweat stays
in the sergeant's cotton shirt.
Two sparrows chase a crow away
from some prize they've hidden in
a nearby sycamore. The crow appears slow.
Sparrows dive and peck between the crow's
wings. The crowd waits as a young soldier figures how
it is you run a knot to make a noose. Bad Joe
stares at his bound hands, moves his thick fingers.
It must be unreal for him—the wet lips
of the few women who never blink, and the men
always taking off their hats and putting them on again.
Two small boy's bodies near the well cast frail
shadows as they collect rocks beside the well.
They drop their rocks into a metal pail.
I turn for home, brush a snail from my failing boot.
It won't rain for a week. Then it will. Some will
say Amen.

These Have Mercy/Have Not

Switchyard for the slow hearted
Blind trackage and empty signal face
Passage toward darkness and horizon
Developments that none can measure
Brick and grease and out there and gear
Garden of whiskey in the brakeman's hands
Stack of creosote soaked railroad ties
Late night track remover and removal
And limit and limiter and operator of horn
Coupling and discard junction, spume
And silence, halo casting worried light
Stalled car, escaped cow, hobo
Wined in his glad sleep
Lithium grease and metal and loose
Noises from the transom, freight
Car in which I will be born
In which I am born, in which
Murder, yield of labor and failure
Tracts of land and tracks across land
And traction, sunlight, empty museum
Noisy heart. Have mercy.

Carnival

It could begin this way. In the café, beside
the busy skirt of the waitress and a steady
sun on the chubby child's head, we'll order eggs
that arrive like broken atoms and coffee dark

and formulaic as all our evenings. We'll sip it hot
and make little remark while – shooting
from the city's center – silver trains and time depart,
point by point, to the far towns

and tired stations of our simple stories. I'll tell you
everything, while hurt cargo passes from Eden
to Nod, and a little boat works the wind, whipping it sick
in the harbor. One yellow sail, small

against the blue world. In a nearer park, a girl discovers
flight through the sudden song of birds, an aging father
counsels his son. Street noise somersaults across cut grass.
City cricket plays his wicked piccolo.

I'll push my empty plate aside and slide my solid hand
across the checkered plastic tablecloth to assure
you: *See? You are you again – flesh and spine – not even
half the ghost you thought you were.*

An Apple for John Clare

He resolved the matter for himself by running away – escaping
– in July 1841…in search of "home" and the hope of being
reunited with his "first wife," Mary Joyce. She had died a
spinster, in 1838. When his family told him of this, he did not
believe them.

– Geoffrey Summerfield

1.

Spring's morning hymn collects
all rain's dialects.
The apple trees come to blossom.
I should have offered an invitation
to a safer century. But instead

I said, Come, John Clare,
to my father's farm. Everything there
performs penance. Here's
the place where you can rest
in the haymow, a plaid blanket over last
year's straw, its small remains.

Through measured rains
this spring, apple blossoms
in our orchard cling.

Point to one and come
October it's yours.
We'll have these three seasons
as winter has the dead.

2.

Dine all summer where you want, John.
Onto your plate happy potatoes tumble
with carrots softened in thick stew.
Sliced bread my mother baked last night
I butter gently so no knife scars its open face.
Enjoy July, John. Take these long days
on your dinner plate. No need to write one thing.

3.

My father downs autumn's last standing hay.
Third cut this good year. See him ride the open-
seat tractor, looking ahead, looking back
at the blades. From high on the orchard hill,
how small he seems, how silent the mower's teeth,
how subtle the tractor at half throttle.
The months here were ours, but, John, the apple
you chose when only a blossom, hangs dark, full
from its short brown stem. I pluck it for you.
Here, winter frosts rough soon. We should be off
by tonight, in search of your first, your best, wife.

Advice for Re-roofing a Small Chapel

Better five shrugs than to give over
when pushed at interview for answer.
Sidestep with something French that sounds
convincingly it could not mean
but does: *I have four toes for ground
and six for happiness almost.*

The wise approach, unless heard—
What? No. No slate deliveries yet. Useless
as I am at flagging down great birds
yelling away, away without us again.

Have some ham. Here. How
it must bother a flasher
in a park. The chill, too
willing the birds go by faster.

Sure you can use this someday sadder.
When asked, of course, but why would anyone?
It's not important as knowing
the French for what does not matter.

*It's one suitable horse for riding, indeed.
But we'll need at least two for any racing to happen.*

Notes from a Journey

We died during a train wreck
outside your winter village
the word *Mary* on our tongues.

Apples. It was apples our mothers
placed in our pale hands.
Apples and smoked ham sticks.
Oranges did not exist then.

We had heard of *Oranges* in our classes
as we had heard of *Elegy* and *Cincinnati*.
Our mothers calmly, terrified, kissed us.

On the platform we were strange
creatures, guarding giant cases
containing our lessons and pants.

We boarded as our belongings
were loaded by thick-wristed men.
Pull and puff went the carriage.

The rest goes crack, goes under.
A young nun points to beads.
The sharp dark, cold water
and far inside, this thought of beds.

Punishment

Fred D'Aguiar

Punishment

When was it I last laughed? I mean really guffawed until my midriff hurt and I cried? There in the jungle washed by star, moon and insect-light. In Jonestown dropped in the middle of the world's biggest garden. The meeting began late at night as usual — Father was a night owl, a late riser who seemed afraid to fall asleep. We sat on aluminum folding chairs arranged in two tight rows of ten, twenty rows deep with a corridor between the two sets of rows. Others, mostly children, squatted on tarpaulin or a spare blanket around the edges of the rows of chairs. All of us faced a plinth covered with cloth and furnished minimally with a small round table on which rested a jug of water, a couple of glasses and Father's much-thumbed, dog-eared bible, and next to the table, a high chair. Father sat in the high-backed chair and looked too small for it, rather than the grand royalty he meant to simulate. He held a microphone with the stand beside him in case he needed to rest the mike and dry his face and take a drink. Mostly there was someone nearby to take the mike and hand him a towel or glass of water. A large fan placed strategically behind him and slightly to the side kept him cool and guaranteed the front rows of the tent would be filled early to garner some of that free air. Bare bulbs burned on long cords strung throughout the corrugated zinc-roofed structure open to the elements on all sides. A generator drowned the insect noises and competed with the arguments of Father booming on the P.A. As stars played hide and seek behind clouds, fireflies flicked their lamps on and off. As the P.A. blasted the dark the multitude of night insects going about their business must have taken in a little of what Father said. Insect-brethren.

He ran his hand through his black hair lifting it off his forehead and slicking the thick, wet mop of it back onto his scalp. He fixed his hard brown eyes on a child seated on the floor with her two siblings and made her squirm. His stare was not vacant but the kind of stare that provided thinking with a framework. He asked her what she thought of her parents who were back in California and agitating to get her, her brother and her sister out of Jonestown. The parents hired lawyers and sent several writs to Georgetown ordering Father to surrender the three children to the authorities. She was a feisty little thing. I nearly slapped her once as was the habit among adults in their dealings with children at Jonestown, for countermanding my instructions during gardening duty. I kept my arm by my side, determined not to be like all the rest. I liked Gina's pluck. Though very thin and short she never failed to hoist up on tiptoe and stick her face into the faces of other children who threatened her. And she willingly gathered plants for me helped by her brother Ben and her sister Clara. Though she was in the middle of them and smallest of the three she ordered both of them around as if she were the eldest. Her sense of herself as the best defender of the family in the absence of her parents persisted though she knew every adult in the Temple was meant to be her new family.

I told her brother and sister and her my Anancy the Spiderman stories, as they were told to me by my father, and as I remembered them or failed to in which case I simply made up the lost details. I storied those children to keep them at their chores and by my side and therefore out of trouble. They, in turn, went on leaf hunting missions for me and brought back stacks of leaves, most known to me but sometimes a few mysteries turned up. Gina — we used first names, knowing that our last name had to be Father's — took the mike from our spiritual and material leader and barked into it so loudly we sat upright and attended her as if freshened by her appearance when, in fact, each of us was near collapse from working all day and listening to him into the small hours. She seemed about nine or ten. I say this because exact ages were anathema in Jonestown, gauged roughly by cosmic events or shared calamities with all birth certificates and such proof of citizenship of our former lives burned, shredded or surrendered to Father and never seen again. I know she had not had her first period and she was spared for this reason from the more arduous chores of womanhood. She held the mike with her right hand and jammed the knuckles of her left hand into her hip. She said about her former parents, "I want to tear them apart, the fuckers. The fucking no-good stirrers. I want to string them up by their fucking heels. Excuse my language, Father," (he nodded for her to proceed), "but I hate those two bitches. They can kiss my ass." She flicked up her dress. She wore nothing under her dress. Her bold gesture brought renewed waves of laughter. "I hope they rot in hell. If they came to get me I would kill them first and then kill myself."

This is where I laughed my loudest. I do not include when I first heard him preach back in California. I cried back then more than I laughed, though it was for joy. This Guyanese jungle setting never rang with so much laughter. If our laughter could harvest fruit the trees would be stripped bare. If our ululating were a season, say the winters back home in the North, then all the land would be covered in snow. I cried with laughter. Everyone howled and clapped and stamped their feet and so the ovation went on long after Gina returned the mike to Father and resumed her place on the floor next to Ben and Clara.

Father called her back to the stage to take a bow and he kissed her on both cheeks and told us she was a child but she should be seen as an example by all of what it takes to be a member of this community and one of his followers.

It takes balls, he said, pointing with the mike at little Gina. And it took a child to show us the kind of balls we need to survive in this place and against all our enemies. My laughter would have subsided were it not for this addendum of Father's – Someone get this child a pair of panties.

This was the last time I really laughed. I am ashamed because I know I laughed for all the wrong reasons. Even as I laughed I knew what should really take the place of laughter I could never show, not in my body. My body could not contain it. I do not mean straightforward tears but a giving over of the body to despair from which there would be no turning back.

In Jonestown no one was allowed to cry without the express permission of Father. Tears at a funeral, fitting. Tears of joy at the height of his sermons, great. Tears of depression or frustration with camp life, not if you valued your skin. I buried my tears face down in my pillow. Look at us in the night and you might wonder why so many of us spent long periods with our faces pressed into the pillow. I am sure I was not the only one who said into my pillow what could never be uttered within earshot of another person and cried and screamed too.

Father stood while he made Gina sit on his throne. He picked up where she left off with warnings about insiders who were now outsiders and perhaps more of a threat than any other person, lawyer or government. He defined those persons as most despicable of all Temple enemies. They knew better and turned their backs on wisdom. They learned all there was to know about the beast and opted to support him and work against the Temple. Gina began to nod off on the throne so the nurse shook her and made her re-join her brother and sister in the audience. Father slumped into the chair and defined lawyers as bloodsuckers, tapeworms, parasites. His speech slurred and he paused for a long time between sentences. He repeated himself and did not seem to know he had said that thing only a moment ago. He repeated it almost verbatim and dwelled on each phrase with the same sense of discovery and revelation.

"A government walks in on us and pretends it cares about us, about how we live but it is here to spy on us, to criticize us, everyone can criticize, and to destroy us. But we will not go away. You hear, that, ears in the night, eyes in the night. A government walks in on us and pretends, pretends it cares. About us. Cares about how we live but it is here to spy on us, to criticize us, everyone can do that, criticize, and it wants to destroy us. But will we go away? No. You hear that, ears on the night, eyes in the ears of the night."

He stopped talking and his head drooped until his chin touched his chest and we knew the night was over because he was over for the night. Sleep for him was death in life, hell on earth, his worst tormentors given free reign with him. So he kept his eyes open and kept us up with him until he had to be carried sleeping in his chair to his bed.

Four men shouldered that throne with Father slumped in it, followed by the nurse and hygienist, both of whom tucked him in. We sat and watched the chair with its precious cargo leave the tent. Only after he was out of sight we moved, scuttled to various sleeping quarters counting on the fingers of one hand how very few hours of darkness remained, how late into the night he talked, so late it was well into the start of another day, and hating the idea of waking before we reached our beds.

We talked about Gina's public outburst for days. It saved her many hours of dull chores and she won a few pairs of decent underwear. Ben and Clara waited on her. That week her name and her brother's and sister's, appeared on the timetable next to mine making me responsible for their personal hygiene. I cut their finger and toe nails, cleaned their ears and combed their hair. I tried to get Gina to deliver a few more nuggets of wisdom but she squirmed and fidgeted like all children subjected to a morning of hair-plaiting and I ended up reprimanding her like all the others. "Keep still, child. How you expect me to tidy your wild head if you keep slipping around like an eel."

"You hurting me."

"If I really hurt you child you would know about it."

To stop myself painting us both into an ugly corner I called her sister and brother over and launched into an Anancy tale. I put aside her night in the spotlight as an aberration.

She remained feisty even when she approached me for a story.

"Do you have any Anancy stories for us today?"

She asked as if I had a store of them on me and it was my duty to give them away before they decomposed because of my neglect and left a bad smell on me. She seemed to think she did me a favor by providing me with a ready and willing audience at no cost to me and at much inconvenience to her going by her folded arms and frown and the slightest trace of a smirk in the corner of her mouth. She was ripe for a slap and when I felt like dishing out a slap to one so young, a common practice here, I knew it was time to conjure Anancy or send her on one of my leaf gathering errands to add to my plant collection. Everyone soon returned to treating Gina like another pair of hands to help me weed the vegetable and herb garden or help reduce the mountain of laundry, dirty dishes and litter. We could not afford to spare her even in her gifted state, the rare gift of talking in the spirit of Father. We needed even her little hands in Jonestown, to stave off the rain and humidity, always a fight against ever-encroaching vegetation which moved faster than I could study it, or come to grips with weeds, and mud when it rained, or from overnight moisture, omnipresent mud from more wet than dry days and never enough hands around.

We made mud pies. We could have cooked with mud. It inveigled its way into everything. The children wore a film of muddy water, their second skin. When I scraped Ben, Clara and Gina's scalps, mud speckled their shoulders and lodged between the teeth of the comb. I brushed the comb with every five strokes on a scalp or rattled it in a basin of water. The children screeched and squirmed without exception and I launched a story to settle them.

I tasted mud too. We salted and peppered it for a flavor other than its mineral promise. The sun baked it and it cracked like the bottom of our feet and the palms of our hands. It squelched when stepped in and grabbed the ankles as if to keep us in it. Patience mud, you will have us all soon enough, so many of us you won't know what to do with us all, where to put us for safekeeping for another day of feasting on us or how to arrange our countless bones other than in a heap.

The children played in water after a downpour. They stripped bare and flung handfuls of mud at each other. They stopped to catch their breaths only to daub mud on each other and waited around like statues for the mud to dry into a cast on them. Mud people. The mud hardened and resembled ashes. They did not want to crack the mud that encased them so the children walked around straight-legged and with arms stuck out beside them, the ghosts of themselves.

We caught them and wanted to beat them for it, for playing dead. Did they not know how hard we fought to free ourselves of mud? They knew and yet they did this mud dance to show us that they did not care to fight the mud but preferred to join forces with it. We scrubbed them hard until they were raw skin and polished bones once again. Do not tempt fate, I told Gina, and Clara and Ben, who followed her and did her bidding. You cannot toy with Death. And they looked puzzled. What? They asked. What did we do? You are playing with fire. This confused them no end. What fire? Clearly mud was nothing like fire.

Gina understood. I threw her my most fierce look, knitted brows, unblinking eyes and pursed lips. She did not do me the honor of looking sheepish like the others. She hardly blinked. I shouted at her more than I reprimanded her two siblings. My look was an order for her to show me a little fear.

Be respectful of me, Gina, or pay a higher price later on. Cleanliness is next to Godliness. Mud on your body is a sign of a corrupt soul. We fight to remove the taste of mud from our mouths, and what do you do? You roll in it. You show us you do not care. We have to walk away from sin, not invite it into our lives.

I wanted to say more, throw in a little science about flesh-eating bacteria and fungus but I stopped myself. I had said too much already. I folded my lips in my mouth and bit on them, tightened them against a spigot of tears. For I heard how much I sounded like one of his sermons and we were full of his sermons, three square meals of them a day and every scrap on our plates chewed thoroughly before we swallowed or else, and every plate spotless. Father fed and full, brimful and near bursting or face Daddy's wrath.

We needed one example of his iron hand, just one. At one of his marathon evening gatherings Father asked just about the most elderly man at the Temple, Old John, why he wanted to go to Georgetown. It was long past midnight and we listened in and out of sleeping upright with our eyes open. A few of us held these false poses of attentiveness and leaned unwittingly by degrees until we had to be nudged upright by someone beside us who we fell against or who wished to spare us the embarrassment of having Father or one of his cohorts shout at us to pay attention.

The mosquito coils dotted everywhere, burned down to stubs. Moths that had earlier jostled each other for room around the light bulbs exhausted themselves and began to drift away. It was at this late hour when our guards were down, I suppose, that the old man, stooped over with rheumatism and osteoporosis, stuttered and said he wanted to see the capital of the country that was his new home before he faced his maker. A few of us even nodded our approval. We could understand that, the last wish of an ancient man. Old John seemed older than the hills. No one among us had memories that predated his existence. We were positive Father would grant it and move on to the next request or case. Old John joined Father from the beginning. Some of us even called him Father, a moniker reserved for our leader. Though crooked in body Old John's long years held out the promise of the durable nature of Father's teachings; that he, Father, could retain the loyalty of Old John for so long was a measure of the enduring truth of his message.

Old John, bent nearly double, waited for an answer. He looked up at Father in a sideways fashion, sticking his chin up. But when Father asked Old John if he would care to tell everyone the real reason why he wanted to go to Georgetown, and not the bullshit excuse of a last rite that might fool some uneducated idiot off the street but was unworthy of an address to his spiritual leader and material provider, a lightning bolt ran through the tent and struck us all to attention.

The old man stooped even more and dropped his chin. Let us hear you, Father bellowed. And with that Father sprang from his seat and thrust the mike into Old John's knobbed hand. "Go on," Father shouted at the top of his voice to compensate for the lack of a mike. He did not seem angry right then, only keen to be heard by everyone. Old John's labored breaths boomed over the P.A. He sighed. The trap could not now be evaded. To deny it would be to call Father a liar; admit to it and he may as well confess to a cardinal sin, that of desertion. We watched him. He seemed even more contorted than before. As he thought through his options each word played on his crumpled spine in jolts of his body. "I can't hear you," Father bellowed. This must be what it was like to think for yourself rather than have Father think for you.

I try to think outside of his teachings and I come up with a blank, a sky empty of stars, moon, cloud, birds. I draw blank, a bulb shining but with no insects to keep it company. No Father, no me. No Father in my head, no head on my shoulders, just a shell for a brain. His words rise up in me and form clouds in my head. Birds sing his praise. Stars paint the sky. I frame them into sentences and I sound like Father, I stick to Father, his sounds for my no-sound brain: an opalescent sky at night, a cloud city drifting by. Old John said, Yes, sir, Father, I wanted to go to Georgetown but now I want to stay here. I have everything that I need or could ever want right here. Don't need no other place. No, sir. Made a mistake in my thinking. I slipped up. Sorry, Father.

And with that the old man fell to one knee and lowered his head. Father jumped off the stage and grabbed the mike from his gnarled hand.

"You slipped up, did you? What do you think would happen to this place if I slipped up? What do you think would happen to each and everyone of you if I caught a little whimsy to go on a jaunt to Georgetown or some other sin bin and maybe never come back? You know what? I do not have to spell it out for you. Your ruin and damnation. Your doom on earth and your doom in hell. You can slip up. I, sir, on the other hand, have no such luxury. You know what happens to people who slip, don't you? Do you?"

"Yes, sir, they fall."

"That's right, they fall. And you, my oldest friend have fallen from a terrible height."

Father beckoned a couple of his helpers over to his side. Two young men of a troop who carry out his physical work, his beatings and lockups, his water immersions and his prolonged verbal assaults for any backsliders, slippers and sliders among us.

"Take him to the well. You will spend the rest of the night in the well."

"Please Jim, no."

"Now I am Jim to you, am I? Your buddy, am I? What happened to Father, Daddy? Take him away. I hope the water will mend your ways."

Father's two lieutenants frog-marched Old John from the tent. His wife, Jemima, a woman even older than his mid-eighties who always hummed hymns while she worked, fainted, and a few women gathered her up and carried her from Congregation Hall as our meeting place was gloriously known. It took a minute of Father shouting at us to pay attention to him and not to the wayfarers in our midst as he referred to Old John and his wife, Jemima, for Father to get us to settle and shake off our involuntary shivers.

His judgment on the old man made me shiver. I belonged to Father, we all did, and this was what he chose to do with us, his children. An army of ants burrowed just below the surface of my skin. I heard

51

nothing for the rest of that night though Father shouted at us and locked eyes with me more than once. I slept with my eyes wide open. I looked awake, open and receptive to Father, but I had shut down all engines in my body, closed all my pores to the world.

My head summoned the catalogue of my plants and a clump of purple-headed lupins poised on a rock revolved in my mind's eye and I sniffed and stroked and peered at it under an imaginary microscope and lifted a sample of it with tweezers and held it to a bright bulb, any and everything to take my mind off Father. I placed Anancy in the country's army, pictured him as a thief, disguised him as a rabbit, fixed him in a pose as the North Star, each leg a ray of light shot from the body of the star, or Anancy caught in a lie and shamed in front of the entire village, or at a banquet and eating humble pie. Plant and Anancy, save me.

My neighbors on both sides of me shook me by the shoulder and nudged my lolloping head until I jumped out of my seat. They carried Father out of the big tent and I could hear him still sermonizing which could only mean I replayed an earlier session of his to compensate for my absence from his current one. I filed out with the rest of the congregation and we tried not to talk about the old man in the well. We kept our mouths shut since it was impossible to know who to trust. Any show of sympathy for him might be reported as opposition to the judgment of Father and no one opposed Father, not within the confines of the camp. I took to my bed but lay in the dark and listened to my breathing and the twists and turns of others settling in for the few hours of grace left before morning. These hours flew by ordinarily. Before we knew it daylight was shaking us in our bed to abandon the Devil, idleness, and rise and shine in the name of the Lord. And so they found me, the chacalaka birds or bush alarm clocks of our settlement, those allotted day-duty, the enforcers who made sure all the beds were vacated by everyone but the infirm, my eyes wide open and still in need of a shake to stir me from my stupor. A handful of mint leaves in my hand, squeezed for their perfume and then kept in my grip through the small hours, the quiet, and then start of dawn life, gripped all night to remind me of something that was still mine.

A part of me held the hand of Old John as they lowered him into the well and the rest of me kept him company throughout the long night of damp bones and cold cramps. From my bed where I lay awake all night, I emptied my eyes into my pillow and my mouth talked into the stuffing to muffle any sound and I curled the rest of the lumpy pillow around my ears to shut out the world of Jonestown. I pictured my body beside Old John's and I told him Anancy stories and he corrected my mistakes. I named the plants that might ease the stiffness in his back and slow down the brittleness of his bones. We talked and cuddled for warmth and in the dark watched each other for the shine in our eyes. And when they pulled him up in the morning and he looked fast asleep and no one could rouse him from his slumber that was because his cold skin and stiff bones told another story for he and I floated down that well and rather than soak all night and freeze we found a portal and squeezed through it and out of this Godforsaken place.

'The Maldon Hawk'

Grevel Lindop

The Maldon Hawk

he let him þa of handon   leofne fleogan
hafoc wið þæs holtes,   and to þære hilde stop

And so, dismissed, I rose on a wingbeat
over horses already scattering to the wood,
unwanted as men turned to their war.
Vassal set loose from his master's service,
blameless outlaw freed to the houseless wild,
circling, I watched thickets of metal and leather
crowd the shallows of the deepening tide.
Now as I scour the air my heart divides
between longing for a man's call and the wideness of the world
where I got honour by my endgame, pleasing nobles
in the hour when the bright dove fled the man-flung hawk.
I pivot at flight's apex but will not return,
though my jewelled eye sees each ring on his corselet
catch sun as he merges into the mass,
death-besotted warriors on their way to darkness.
Gladly I would stoop a last time into his language
but already battle's whirlpool sucks him in, his face downward,
nameless and eyeless among the iron helmets.
I am a word forgotten from his story.
He is a landmark fading from my sight.
Men had seemed to have some special knowledge:
now the sea-wind tastes of death, they rush towards it –
whether to sing with saints or feast with battle-fellows
or lie at a tree's root until the world ends
they know no better than I. Never again,
child of the waste moor and the tufted woodland,
will I perch on that wrist, grasp the bone beneath.

'Terrestrial Variations'

Jane Griffiths

Terrestrial Variations

Somewhere there's a life where we never left the mountains,
where we sleep each night under ridges whose snow drifts

in open books – white, white and unimpressed.
Our dog's long shadow slopes across the page I'm writing.

Somewhere we kissed at seventeen, somewhere
we sleep without dreaming. Between us snow drifts

light as the sun's power of suggestion
in an empty room. Do you know that feeling? –

the line between your lives so thin you could cross it
and back again, the way a key springs in the ignition.

Somewhere you're a medic in Brisbane and we mean
different things when we say *the mountains, the coastline.*

Somewhere I've a small-holding in New Hampshire;
somewhere we're godparents to each other's children

(and on our mobiles, off the radar whole afternoons).
Somewhere the static on the radio speaks in tongues,

our daughter maps her name onto *the world, the universe.*
Somewhere my car was totalled and we never met.

Somewhere I'm writing this to ask if you won't spring
that key and head south through the mountains,

the foothills, the stubborn interference in the ether –
though the satellite above it all's just the same old moon,

won't you come here, now, and in the singular?

A Malady of the Heart

Sabyn Javeri-Jillani

(Extract from a novel in progress, *Once We Were Beautiful*)

A Malady of the Heart

Hakim Dilbar's clinic was an immaculate square of white paint in the midst of a crumbling, dilapidated building. *'Bismillah Ur Rahman Ur Rahim'*, 'Enter, in the name God,' was written on the door and above it a little sign jutted out of the wall like a tiny flag. 'Hakim Dilbar, *Mahir-i-Nafsiyat aur Dard-i- Dil'*. 'Experts in problems of the mind and maladies of the heart'. Practitioners since the court of Nawab Siraj-ud Daulah -- the last of the great Mughal kings.

The sign never failed to impress me. It was nearly twenty years since I first accompanied Ami Jan to the Hakim's clinic but I still felt that mixture of awe and dread that I did as a child. As our troop of mother, daughter, grandson and Ayah descended from the car, a vendor selling mud toys approached. *'Matti kay khilona!* Unbreakable mud toys, try it, buy it, try it, buy it, mud toys!'

Zahid's small face cheered up at the sound of the man's weary call. 'Mummy can I have some?'

'Aihai! You can have the entire cart my little Baba,' Halima answered before me. 'Just you wait here and I'll get them for you.'

'No, I want to choose myself.'

'Come then, but don't show any excitement. You don't know these rascals. The minute you like something they double the price. Now listen. Whichever one you like, say "Ugh! that one is the worst". Understand?'

Zahid nodded though I could see he didn't.

As soon as the vendor approached, his nasal voice created a melancholic atmosphere. 'Ah look at this kettle, once a beautiful kettle, still a beautiful kettle, look at its cup, unbreakable mud cup!'

Zahid squealed as he saw the mud animals. 'That one! I want that one!'

The vendor allowed himself the slightest of smiles and promptly said, 'Oh little Baba you have the taste of a prince. That one is the most exquisite.' He quickly placed the toy in Zahid's hands. 'Just one red note, it costs.'

'Oho you rascal, do you think I was born yesterday?' Halima said.

The man, missing the metaphor, looked at Halima's wrinkled face in horror.

'Don't try to fool us with exquisite craftsmanship-partnership whatever. Quote the right price or take your sweaty face and roam the streets of Karachi for the rest of the afternoon. Arre who plays with these mud toys nowadays anyways? As it is, our Zahid Baba has toys which can talk, walk, even a little dog that can do backflips. Have you ever seen such a thing even in your dreams you miserable mud toy seller? One red rupee my foot!'

The vendor, who wore a dark brown shalwar kameez stained with huge patches of sweat, shifted his yellow turban and said, 'Look at the workmanship Bibi, it takes my wife six hours to make one toy.'

'Take it or leave it, we'll give you a ten.'

'Wah, Ya Allah, what justice is this? I ask for one hundred and you wave a tenner at me.'

He reached out to take the toy back and Zahid shrank back. Halima, offended by the man's front, smacked his hand with her Chinese fan. 'Oye, stop this daylight robbery and tell us a reasonable price.'

'The price is reasonable,' the man said.

My patience was wearing thin and if I'd had any money on me at all I would have thrown it at the man's face by now. I looked at Ami Jan but she seemed lost again, oblivious to the racket around her. I watched silently as Halima went on bargaining while Gul Khan and Zahid moved their necks to and fro between the vendor and Halima as if they were watching a tennis match. Finally an agreement was reached and our procession resumed towards the white sterile walls of the doctor Sahib's clinic. Inside, a wall portioned the room in to two neat halves.

Halima and Ami Jan and I were admitted in one side of the waiting hall while Gul Khan and Zahid were told to wait in the other half reserved for males.

'Hai hai!' Halima exclaimed. 'But our child is hardly four years old. Why can't we bring him into the women's quarters.'

'Aye Bibi!' the receptionist, a fat woman whose flesh spilled off the steel stool she sat on, straightened the duppatta over her orange henna stained hair, then spitting a thin red arc of chewed beetlenut juice into a silver spittoon said, 'Even a pregnant woman is not allowed here in the Zenana half, lest she be carrying a male and he stains the purity of other women's purdah. The Doctor Sahib's faith is very pure as you know, and who knows perhaps it's this strictness of belief that has bestowed upon him such powers of healing.' Ami Jan nodded, suitably impressed, while Halima just smacked her forehead with her palm.

It was decided that instead of waiting out in the car, Gul Khan would drive Zahid back to Shiraz's parent's house while we would make our way back home by taxi should we become free sooner.

And so the wait began. We sat down on a hard cold bench that reminded me of the classrooms of the primary school I had attended. I watched the patients disappear one by one into the gaping white hole that was the curtain that separated the Hakim's clinic from the waiting room, until it was finally our turn.

Hakim Dilbar was a delicate man. There was, I thought no other word but delicate to describe his fragility. Nearing ninety he sat cross-legged on a divan, his hands resting loosely on the sides. He wore a snow white Kurta Pyjama that seemed to have been woven out of the softest of threads. His white beard, white hair and unusually pallid eyes contrasted further by the darkness of his pupils seem to give him a ghostly ethereal appearance. If it wasn't for the red rose in his button hole and the strong smell of *Itar* perfume that drifted from his person I would have dismissed him as another one of my visions.

Ami Jan pushed me down gently by the shoulders onto the silver metal stool while she sat on the chair nearby. Halima squatted down on the floor beside the Hakim Sahib's throne as if it was just another visit to a relative's house. Fixing her duppatta that kept sliding off her near bald head, she began to talk about how her troubles were causing her to lose all her hair and how was it that a man as ancient as the Hakim himself managed to have a full crop? 'After all, men are more prone to baldness no?' Ami Jan's cheeks coloured and she quickly motioned Halima to keep quiet. Thinking better, she briskly told her to wait outside.

'Sometimes they say sit down, sometimes they say get up! Arre no one thinks about my poor knees, how they suffer from your indecision!' Halima grumbled. 'Aie Hakim Sahib, give the begum some medicine too. She keeps losing her mind and can't make up her memories!'

'Losing her memory and unable to make up her mind,' I corrected.

By now thoroughly embarrassed, Ami Jan hissed at her to get out. The faintest of smiles appeared on the old man's face as Halima lifted the bamboo curtain and stood outside. I smiled, unsure if she was guarding the entrance or straining to listen.

'Please excuse her Hakim Sahib,' Ami Jan said. 'Halima doesn't realise what she's saying. But she's been with the family for so long...'

Just then a rumbling voice sounded as someone cleared his throat. It was then that we noticed the other man. While the elder Hakim sat on the throne-like divan looking like a king observing his court, his son, a younger version of the Hakim except for the labcoat and spectacles, sat hunched in a corner on a small white desk behind a large open register and a row of glass bottles filled with tiny pills and forbidding looking herbs.

'Name?' he asked without looking up at us.

We were too taken in by the second man's presence to answer quickly. The elder Hakim spoke, in a voice that seemed to have been dipped in a mixture of sugar and honey and woven like a basket of banana leaves. 'He means which one of you is the patient?'

For some reason the question made me smile, the smile spread further and a giggle came out. Where had I heard that mad men always thought it was the world around them that had become insane? Looking at Ami Jan's alarmed face as I laughed, I could see that she thought I was the lunatic.

Nafas,' said the elder Hakim asking for my wrist.

While the younger version pottered about with stethoscopes and charts, the Elder calmly leaned back and taking my pulse with his thumb and forefinger closed his eyes. When he opened them again I stared at him and asked, 'What can you see by checking my pulse that he can't with all his instruments?' Ami Jan hushed me at my impertinence but the Elder just smiled. He had a strange smile. Only one half of his mouth lifted while the other half remained stern, the corners pointing downwards. It unnerved me to think that Papa's once full grin had been reduced to a similar smirk.

'Sometimes,' he said scanning my face, 'the stream of our pulse carries the illness into those dark forgotten corners of our bodies where the doctor's tool cannot reach.'

'Come here *Beti*,' he leaned forward.

I shifted in my stool.

'*Ajijazat hai?*' He asked my mother for permission.

'Proceed,' she replied.

I had heard tales of how some of these spiritual healer type people beat out spirits from the body, how the skin had been burned to release a trapped ghost and how they tore out your nails to remove the impurities that crawled through the opening. I shivered as I thought what would they do to someone who saw visions?

He held my face close to his. So close that I was breathing his breath. Before I could open my mouth to protest, he flicked my eyelid inside out.

'No!' I screamed not so much from the pain but from the unexpectedness of it all.

'Hmmm,' he mumbled. 'The secret thrives…'

'What is it Hakim Sahib?' Ami asked, clasping her chest.

'What do you mean what is it? They haven't even asked us why we are here,' I said.

'It is a malady of the heart,' came the Hakim's verdict.

'A malady of the heart?' repeated Ami Jan.

'A malady of the heart?' echoed Halima from behind the curtain.

'A malady of the heart,' sighed the son, closing the register with a thump as if admitting failure and putting away his charts and vials.

When we had recovered from the resounding noise, Ami Jan asked, 'Surely, Hakim sahib, with your powers there must be a cure?'

Hakim Sahib ran his fingers through his long white beard and began fingering his beads. When he spoke, his voice was low and measured.

'The heart is the main connector of the body. It is through the heart our body pumps blood, our spirit becomes purified and it is through the heart that our desires become tainted.'

He looked sharply at me, 'The heart is vital but the heart is not supreme. We must remember we control it and not the other way around. The heart that does not listen becomes a danger to the self.'

As if in protest, my heart began to beat loudly against my chest. *Thump, thump, thump*, I felt as I if I were standing naked with my breasts exposed, my nipples ripped out and only an unruly blood stained organ thumping itself into a slow hollow beat.

'How much does he know?' I felt myself asking for the second time.

The sun seemed harsh and unforgiving after the soft haze of the clinic. I blinked, squinted and rolled my eyes around, assuring myself that my lids still worked. As I looked sideways I noticed the alarmed look on Ami Jan's face. Suddenly I felt a softening inside my unruly heart. I was all she had, this woman. Me and God, and perhaps Halima.

We stood, the three of us, silently beside each other. Three comically sad women with ill-behaved hearts that refused to listen. Me, Ami Jan and Halima -- failures at the game of love. What must we look like to passers-by, I wondered? Lost wanderers searching for an address, newly discharged patients or three possessed women hoping for a cure, the evil witches of Macbeth, or just three ordinary women waiting for a rickshaw. The thought amused me and I began to laugh. But perhaps combining the laughter with an eye roll was not such a good idea for Ami Jan began to cry softly and Halima too blew her nose in her *duppatta*. But her approach to sadness was different. 'Arre that cursed driver, if only he had returned by now, we wouldn't have to wait in this horrid heat for a ride home!' Halima began to speak loudly, pulling Ami Jan under the shade of a lone tree littered with advertisements. Following them into the shade, I rested my forehead against the cool trunk reading aloud the colourful advertisements.

'Do you think you are going mad?' I read out. 'Think you are going to die? Get rid of the evil eye, come to Baba G, come today, don't be shy.' I walked over to the next ad. 'Has your manhood let you down? Contact Hakim Hikmat, sole distributor of the German Mr. Lover Lover Bombastic syrup.' I read slowly, my tongue feeling foreign around the Urdu script I hadn't read for eleven years. 'Are you no longer in control? Contact the Sayana Buddhu, expert in Bangal Ka Jaadu.' And then beneath a drawing of a heart split in two, there was a number and an address. 'For the Broken-Hearted,' it read. 'You break it -- we mend it,' said the slogan that ran all around the trunk in three tiers.

A sniffling Ami Jan trailed anxiously after me while I went round the tree reading the series of advertisements as if unwinding a string. Halima chattered away as if nothing was wrong.

'Halima, stop a Taxiwallah. No use waiting around for the driver at an unsafe time like this,' Ami Jan said pulling her *duppatta* tighter around her face.

'Alright Begum Sahiba. As you say, but don't forget to tell off that useless driver for not showing up on time!'

'Maybe he got held up in traffic, Halima. After all, it was our fault that we brought Zahid along. Poor man had to go all the way to drop him then come back to pick us. Don't be so harsh on him all the time.'

'Arre traffic my foot! Probably he is having potato samosa on the beach right now with that equally useless sweeper girl Rani! Always ready to blacken their faces, those two are. I say it is all your leniency, Begum Sahiba.'

'Oof, enough Halima, now please just go and get us a taxi,' Ami Jan replied pressing her temples with her forefinger and thumb.

'Alright, I'll go! *Humara kya hai, hum to nokar hai.* After all, I'm just a servant, what say do I have?'

'What more is left to say now, Halima,' Ami Jan seethed.

'Fine, fine, I was just saying,' Halima replied.

Just then a yellow cab rounded the car and I quickly flagged it down, thinking that perhaps I was of some use to them afterall, when Halima barged ahead of me.

'How much to Society?'

'It is metered cab, Bari Bi,' replied the driver.

Oh no, I thought, here we go again.

'Arre old woman be your wife! I don't understand this meter sheter. I'll give you a Tenner and that's it. Take it or leave it.'

The man rolled up his window and left.

'Halima,' Ami Jan said raising her voice to the loudest I had heard in a long time. 'Have you gone completely mad? How can you bargain at a time like this? How can you even think about it when the city is being slaughtered like a meathouse?'

'Arre Begum Sahib, another one will be along in a short while. All is well. Just stay calm,' Halima replied a little sheepishly.

All around us the city was dug up and little hills of sand stood like miniature pyramids. Dug up roads, abandoned pipes, broken electricity poles, half constructed buildings, some pockmarked by bullet holes, made the city looked like a bombed out war zone. Yet people walked about or stood like aimless cattle watching, chewing toothpicks, picking their nostrils or twirling their moustache. Some like Gul Khan twirled their waistbands. A few women stood at the junction which was now an unofficial bus stop. A cue of donkey carts, cars and bikes formed behind a bus that skidded to a sudden stop, blocking the mouth of the roundabout and causing angry shouts. A man wearing a dark shalwar suit stained darker by the sweat patches on his back and chest descended and slammed the side of the bus as men quickly clambered inside and when there was no more room left to squeeze inside, they climbed onto the roof, squatting like stubborn monkeys. The few women wrapped their headscarves closer to their skulls and with downcast eyes got in next to the driver. Now the man slammed the side of the bus and shouted, '*Jannay dey,* Let's go, Let's go!' running along with the bus as it picked up speed. 'Lets go,' he shouted one final time before clambering aboard just as the bus lurched forward letting out a puff of smoke, its creaking body permanently tilted to the left and painted with colourful slogans and pictures.

I was so immersed in the whole rigmarole of the bus that I didn't notice Halima hailing an Auto-rickshaw. The man stopped a few feet away and when Halima stubbornly refused to walk over, tapping her feet impatiently, he reversed puffing smoke and black leather flaps each painted with an eye, right into our faces. '*Bori nazar walay tera mu kala.*' 'May you blacken your face if you put an evil eye on me,' read the slogan on its back. As we walked around to its front I noticed several more, 'Look but with Love,' being the most prominent one as it was painted in bold red lettering and a pair of eyes winking were drawn underneath. Inside on the red patent flaps a poster of the Punjabi film actress Saima had been glued, her heavy cleavage spilling out of the too tight sari blouse nearly accosting us as we struggled to get inside the small vehicle. 'Once you come inside me you'll never want leave!' read the sign inside the rickshaw placed strategically underneath the poster of the voluptuous actress. I could see Ami Jan's cheeks aflame as her glance fell upon the double meaning. Halima who was the last one to get in, unable to read, remained blissfully ignorant and chatted happily, 'Aren't you glad Begun Sahiba we didn't get into that *looteray* Bank robber's taxi. After all, why pay so much for such a short distance anyway? Rickshaws are a far better option!'

After twenty minutes of jostling against the steel pipes of the rickshaw and the impertinent breasts of Saima the actress, I could no longer stand the rickshaw driver's smirk in the rear-view mirror. Ami Jan sat so stiff and rigid that I wondered if she had turned to stone. Even Halima seemed slightly subdued tolerating the rickshaw driver's lewd stare and tuneless humming to the cheap and distasteful Bollywood songs he was playing on a cassette player that dispelled more static than music. At first I thought it was Ami Jan's scolding that had finally had some effect on her, but later I realized that it was the small picture of the political leader Altaf Hussein on the windshield that had got her tongue. Altaf Bhai and I had something in common. We had both been banished to London and now continued to live there in self-exile. But while I was powerless and isolated, Altaf Bhai managed to wield the power of his sword over the city with ruthless cynicism and a deadly following. His supporters feared no one and in turn everyone feared them. I had heard that even the Army was helpless against them and watched with averted eyes their lootings and killings all over the city.

When we surprisingly stopped at a red-light, a little boy selling newspapers flashed one in our face. "Stop Press! Benazir's murderer spotted. Killer framed in full close up! Buy your copy before it sells out.

News Flash, News Flash, Benazir's murderer spotted. Stop Press!'

Eagerly I reached out for a copy leaving Halima to haggle over the price. Fresh images of Benazir's blood, as dark as the nail varnish that had spilt on the carpet the day of her death, flashed through my mind as I scanned the broad sheet. I turned it over searching for a name, for a face. But all I saw was a silhouette of a nameless man, circled loosely. This blurry, hazy shadow was the killer. I let out a laugh surprising not only Ami Jan and Halima but also the Rickshaw driver who's been driving with his head turned around to catch a glimpse of the paper. 'What does it say? Who killed her?'

'This nameless blob,' I answered.

As two heads bent over the page and one leaned over the divide, I pointed to a dark shadow of a man pulling a pistol so close to the back of Benazir's head, that if she had turned around at that instant she would have bumped right into him.

By the time we reached home, even Halima's haggling was half-hearted and she let Ami Jan pay the full fare with lacklustre grumbling as she dragged her feet inside. 'So expensive everything has become these days,' she mumbled. 'Prices are touching the sky…'

'Nothing is cheap in this country,' said the Riskhaw driver pocketing the money into the folds of his *shalwar*.

'Except human life,' added the gardener who was tying up the leaves he'd raked earlier into sacks. 'They'll kill you for a mobile phone down where I live.'

As I got out of the rickshaw, the driver asked me for the paper. 'Since you have read it,' he added.

I hesitated, finding some strange perverse comfort in having a real person associated with her sudden unnatural death. He reached out for it and before I could respond he grabbed it out of my hand, lingering for a second on my fingers. With a firm grasp on my wrist Ami Jan pulled me away, her eyes fixed on the picture of Altaf Hussain plastered on the Rickshaw.

'Tch, tch,' we heard him mutter as he scanned the paper. 'As if the first attempt on her life hadn't been enough to teach her a lesson. No, she had to come back for seconds, this Madam did. Now look where it got her! And what good was her death to us? Complete shutdown in the country for full five days! Where is a day-wager to go? My eight children and two wives starved for the five days that I couldn't pick up any fares. All because of that Madam Democracy.'

The gardener came over and asked to see the paper. Satisfied, he nodded. 'What can you do Brother? Women don't think with their heads. They are impulsive creatures, good for running the house but not a country! After all, politics is not shopping.'

'Right you are, Brother. They don't have the brains,' said the rickshaw driver, revving up the motor. 'Women, they only listen to their hearts.'

Poems

Alice Willington

Iconostasis

The way up Belukha is the glacier,
its rocks lifted and turned
into uneven scarps. It seeps
at its terminus into untouchable Eden,
a lake of jade.
We hammered steel into snow
and ice, as if carving out
a dream of mountaineers
in one night's sleep.

              Dislodged,
it fell away, until the walls
of the tent were a curtain
before the planets, the arched icons.
I dreamed the sun, the moon
and Jupiter eclipsed,
each one of us isolated and split.
In unbearable brightness
I climbed the cathedral.

Alice Willington

Harpkeys

The bones of my ears were restrung,
a radio broadcasting a night
moored off the sea-caves.

The malleus fell on the dip of oars
and the strain of the rowlocks,
your stealth, your breath, drawing near

to the halls of water held
in the incus, the waves of my blood
lifting and crashing, lifting and crashing

until dawn, the song of the thrush
cantering the stapes to the caverns of the air,
the beached vibrations.

Dusk

The night mist dusts the garden
with deepening form. The roses shimmer,
hedges move and retreat on the path,
on the surface of water. We emerge
and disappear, coral fish, mirages.

The gravel under my feet whispers
and rolls, uncertain whether to call.
We are turning in the paths
and the ends of the maze,
our shadows a film on hornbeam.

I have darkened my lips to dulled blood
for you to catch my skin in moonlight.
The roses are closing in on the path.
My hair tumbles, the cut of my dress
shudders on the ground.

The Long Corridor

It's here again, or I've come back
into the long corridor of partitions
and the silence of *no one else there*,
stepping away from the new moon
letting itself in at the window,
the board with chopped garlic.

It comes as stealth tide
in through the back door of the kitchen,
bringing with it a choking
or asking, *Is anyone there?*
It is Saturday night in the dormitory rooms
and the party elsewhere.

If I turned up would they stare
across the balconies,
faces like flat moons?
It is evening without windows
and the garlic cooked sour,
an absence of footsteps close as horses.

Late Supper

The garlic is fresh,
a new script.
The tomatoes are blanched
to free their skins.

The sun lowers itself
into the armchair of the dusk
and comes into the kitchen
asking for whisky.

I hold the bottle up to the light,
watch its colour lift
from peat to the amber pearls
of a necklace.

I am unable to imagine
what is going to happen.
I lay the knife against the clove,
slip its edge between flesh and skin.

It is as if the trees had not
hunched down into night
but released their sap
on the crush of each other.

Eve

Eve is out this afternoon
everywhere, like caterpillars
in the sun,
           easily found
if looked for,
her markings a flash
of paradise flowers.

Eve lifts her camera,
adjusting the shadow
of leaves,
           the no-colour
of the fountain,
its slants and absence
a distinct seeking.

Eve finds Eve
under the ash and the brim
of her hat.
           Nowhere else
for her but here,
the tulips camouflage
for her shirt and eyes.

Eve photographs Eve
in bluebell, magnolia,
blouse and jeans,
           her brown hair
over her face,
closed flesh. The man still
in a deep sleep.

Mirage

The ink blooms in water,
    words spill unformed,
  for a second
        another language
          speaks
   in the currents
   and swirls
of the taste of coffee and apple smoke
        as a cloud on the tongue,
   before water
     breaks up the intruder
   into its letters.

When you dip your hand
  into the bowl
the indigo separates the rain
        on the beech leaves
   from robes
     swept over the face
    against sand's annihilation
        of kohl
  and the desert's unexpected cold,
     pale blue
on the ridges of your fingers,
         a script
   untiled and moving
     into sound.

Starlight

(Eddington proved Einstein's Theory of General Relativity
by photographing the stars during an eclipse)

The stars do not align on the plates.
It takes Spain to miss Israel – Guy
tells me that *hola* is *Allah*, a filament
of sky between the same star, the same
white stone and dust.

Between the columns of the Mezquite
there is silence. Words overlay words
in prayer mesmeric as carpet silk,
as if gravity has pulled my sight
beyond darkness

to blue sky over terraced syllables
of *hola, Allah*. Lines of olives
graceful as arches, the same photograph
is taken again as the sun's mass
bends the stars.

What's Lost

Paula Bardowell Stanic

What's Lost

"...People shouldn't be able to walk into you and
smash you and... just walk on."

Debra wants a simple remembrance for her daughter Rudi. Alex
thinks they should provoke change and husband Lenny just
wants to forget. Having missed the funeral, Gina finally
turns up a year late. Amid recurring memories, news reports
and intensifying relations, each walks in and out on each
other, struggling to make their own way and sense of an
increasingly troubled time.

The following extract is taken from the opening scenes.
Gina's last meeting with her 17 year old niece Rudi before
her death and Gina's first contact with her sister Debra a
year later. (Having missed Rudi's funeral)

Notes on text

/ means the next line comes straight in.
... a struggle for a word or thought.
Character's name no dialogue means a deliberate silence from
that character.

"What's Lost" won the 2008 Alfred Fagon Award. Rehearsed
reading Royal Court Theatre (downstairs) 3th December 2008

Prologue - A Memory.

> *RUDI'S room. Music plays as RUDI 17 talks*
> *intensely to GINA 40. They share a spliff.*
> *GINA'S head hangs between her legs.*

Rudi   So these three...well, kids, just kids. They
        walk into Top Shop. And everyone looks, cause
        they're... loud, really and you know, there's
        something, they don't look... Can't be more than
        twelve, thirteen. But they're wearing, you know,
        not the usual Kate Moss on a budget gear. Bits
        but they've not got it. Wouldn't look if you
        couldn't hear them. Wouldn't notice

> *GINA takes a couple of deep breaths.*

Rudi   Drugs, too many drugs, maybe.

Gina   I can't take what I used to.

> *GINA brings her head up.*

Gina   Much as I try.

> *RUDI thinks before continuing.*

Rudi   The second they step in, you know it, know some
        ...collision's coming. Security man's on them.
        They just stare him out. Blank, blank looks.
        Make a show of picking things up, carrying
        them about, chucking them. You know, you see,
        feel but you can't...what can you, you
        just...watch.

> *RUDI stops and thinks.*

Rudi   Go downstairs, try to get into another space
        but, you know, I'm just listening out. Wandering
        by racks of shoes, rails of glittering outfits,
        through bags all this useless, useless stuff

Rudi   that means nothing you know? Cause something's going to kick off and...where will we all be after?

> *GINA takes a long, deep drag. She watches the smoke disintegrate in the air.*

Rudi   Start to think it's one of those imagined moments, except it's that...quiet as I start back up the stairs, that weird 'it's waiting' quiet.

Gina   What?

Rudi   As I get closer to the top I feel the change, smell the panic. The commotion, this thing we'd all been waiting for has past. Past us, not him. See the face of the security guard who winked at me as I came in. He's collapsed on the floor with this face... his arm's turned the wrong way, all...out of line with his body. People crowd. We're all just there, present. And I don't want to be one of them, gathered, involved, now. So I walk.

Gina   That's fucking awful.

Rudi   Sound rises behind me, sort of respectful. Everyone working together, now it's over. Disaster's past and hasn't taken any of them. But he's lying there, maybe dead, maybe. For taking his job seriously or too seriously or just for doing it. He's lying there all collapsed, bent for trying to protect, what? And we're cowards or clever. Them, what did they get? And how are they so...convinced of their right to it, that they knock out whatever's in their way?

Gina   *(GENUINLY)* Shop down Camden. You know who's who in Camden.

Rudi   See these moments everywhere. Not confined to Hackney or Harlesden.

Gina   Yeah. World's got scarier.

Rudi   Made me think.

           Short pause.

Rudi   Thought maybe I'd volunteer on this project?
          Help out with these workshops they have or
          something, but/

Gina   Great.

Rudi   Mum/

Gina   Come round/

Rudi   She expects/

Gina   Just go for it/

Rudi   focus.

           GINA smiles to herself.

Gina   Focus.

Rudi   Too young to help other youth.

           Beat.

Gina   You just need to access yourself.

Rudi   Says I need to concentrate.

Gina   Have a few years out.

Rudi   Few years head down she says.

Gina   Don't want to be one of those who never move
          outside their usual existence.

           Beat.

Rudi   Yeah.

Gina   How many trillions of miles is the planet?
Don't feel it here, move.

Rudi   Yeah.

Gina   Staying one place isn't normal. Dee should get
that. Our parents did.

Rudi   ...Sometimes I just sit working it all through.
What do you do?

Gina   What you can.

Rudi   Maybe.

> *Pause.*

Gina   What time is it?

Rudi   Don't worry.

> *GINA smiles at her.*

Gina   You should be out with your mates.

Rudi   You're a mate, sort of.

Gina   Older than your mother.

Rudi   So?

Gina   Leather me if she walks in.

Rudi   Told you/

Gina   Always pops up, pops out to catch me doing
the wrong thing.

Rudi   She won't

Gina   Be struck off for this

Rudi   She's working late.

Gina   Probably receives messages via satellite?

Rudi   She doesn't need technology.

            Beat.

Gina   Lenny about?

Rudi   He's fine, smokes himself.

Gina   ...Yeah?

Rudi   Found a bag in his pocket once.

Gina   Won't stop the moralist breaking out if he
            spots you.

Rudi   He understands stress.

Gina   Stress now is it?

            RUDI gives her a look.

Rudi   I do it all the time.
            She walked in once. Smelt it. Just said I was
            burning herbs.

            GINA smiles to herself.

Rudi   Meditative herbal stuff.
            Should've just been honest.

Gina   Where would that get you?

Rudi   I'm seventeen. I can take it.

            Beat.

Gina   You don't, do you, smoke all the time?

Rudi   Don't try to be mum.

            GINA looks at her for a moment.

Gina   Just trying to be a decent aunty, once.

            Pause.

> *RUDI stares at GINA.*

Gina What?

Rudi Nothing.

> *Silence.*

Rudi Maybe I could come to Brighton with you, for a bit.

> *Beat.*

Gina Haven't you got things to sort here, college, all that stuff?

Rudi All done.

Gina Well yeah, maybe

Rudi Be good.

Gina ...yeah in a couple of weeks. Give me time to get back and sorted.

Rudi Two of us on the beach, looking out at the sea at night.

Gina Barely go down anymore.

Rudi Be great.

Gina Went down one time, looked out it was murky.
Leaden. Full of floating shit.
Cans, paper, cigarette butt type shit.
Who throws fag ends in the sea?

Rudi ...

> *Beat.*

Gina Yeah. Come, come up.

Rudi Next week?

Gina   Date.

              Pause.

Rudi   You know, sometimes I think I'll never find a
              face attractive enough to kiss.

Gina   Relax hon.

              GINA gives her a big kiss on the head.

Gina   You will.

              The room falls apart.

              Scene 1 - GINA & DEBRA.

RUDI'S ROOM. (One year on) A messy looking GINA stands
a bit out of it, looking at the stripped room. DEBRA 38,
efficiently dressed and mannered stands behind her. GINA
is uneasy in her presence.

              Long silence.

Gina   I keep/

Debra   She wasn't shot

Gina   I know/

Debra   It wasn't a gun

Gina   No/

Debra   Nothing to do with shooting.

Gina   Just...what I see/

Debra   Not a gangsta moment.

Gina

Debra	Just a pathetic little knife in the hands of a scared childish child.
Gina	I know Dee/
Debra	Then why do you insist on dreaming different?
Gina	That's not/
Debra	Turning it into a myth
Gina	No/
Debra	No?
Gina	Just...what goes round my head.
Debra	Should get it checked
Gina	It's normal/
Debra	Strange/
Gina	Considering...

> *Beat.*

Debra	Considering.

> *GINA turns to face DEBRA. They stare at each other. They are incredibly still until GINA breaks.*

Gina	It's good to see you. Really, really good.
Debra	Yes.
Gina	Lost weight.

> *DEBRA tuts.*

Gina	What?
Debra	...Everyone thinks it's fine to comment on my appearance.

Gina   Not seen you... that's all.

            Silence.

Debra   How come?

Gina   What?

Debra   You came, now

Gina   I/

Debra   Nothing going on in Brighton?

Gina   Brighton's over.

Debra   Right.

Gina   Anyone with imagination moves on after a
            couple of years.

Debra   And your art?

Gina   Having a break... holiday.

Debra   Won't be the next Chris Ofili then?

Gina   I'm an animator

Debra   ...Disney?

Gina   *(GENTLY)* Don't pretend you don't understand
            what I do.

            Silence.

Debra   So/

Gina   You stripped the room.

Debra   It is almost a year.

Gina   A year

Debra   The longest

Gina	Yeah

Silence.

Gina	Sorry/
Debra	Did you want to stay?
Gina	...If it's alright.
Debra	Money?

Beat.

Gina	You know
Debra	The artist's life.
Gina	...Thinking of moving back.
Debra	Here?
Gina	Thinking
Debra	Permanently?
Gina	See how it feels.
Debra	Expensive.
Gina	Everywhere's going that way.
Debra	Most of us are trying to get out.
Gina	Everywhere's going the same.
Debra	Is it?

Beat.

Gina	Just need a place, space for a week, two.
Debra	Yes.

Gina   And, to be here, with you, Lenny.
           Where is he, work?

Debra   Away.

Gina   Away?

Debra   Yes.

                 GINA stares at her.

Gina   I'm sorry/

Debra   What would you do with the flat?
           If you, escape.

                 Long beat.

Gina   I need...change.

Debra   Yes, I need a bit of that.

Gina   Thinking about a few things

Debra   Nice.

Gina   Might go off somewhere Cuba, Mexico
           somewhere...warm.

Debra

Gina   Just a thought.

Debra   It's good. I would. If there was the chance.
           Escape.

Gina   Come.

                 DEBRA smiles at her.

Gina   Come.

Debra   ...

Gina   We could do a road trip.

Debra   Do people really do those?

Gina   Come

Debra   I can't

Gina   You've never just taken off.

Debra   No time.

Gina   Take some.

Debra   I have a lot on.

Gina   It'll help

Debra   No.

            Short pause.

Debra   Be okay in here tonight?

            GINA looks around the room.

Gina   Next door'll do. Settee's fine.

Debra   I'm up late, some nights

Gina   Me too.

Debra   Most nights.

Gina   Sit up together, watch some late night TV.

Debra   I have people coming over to help with plans.
            Don't know what time we'll finish.

Gina   ...Probably be out late anyway. Catch up with
            things, see what's happening.

Debra   So in here is okay?

            Beat.

Gina   Fine.

Beat.

Debra   I'm organising a remembrance.

Gina   I know.

Debra   One year.

Gina   I'll help. If I can?

> *DEBRA starts to leave.*

Debra   I'll get you bedding.

Gina   Beat me, kick me, pull my hair, scream, something. Something.

> *DEBRA just stares at her.*
> *GINA goes over and embraces her tightly.*
> *The moment is awkward for both but GINA holds it.*

Gina   I'm sorry.

> *DEBRA pats her and gently slips out of her hold.*

Debra   Yes.

> *DEBRA leaves. GINA watches her go.*
> *She looks around the room, listens out.*
> *She takes out her mobile, checks it for messages.*
>
> *Blackout.*
>
> *Music.*

'Love Story'

David Constantine

Love Story

Head of the valley or his head, all one –
He had come there hunted, though the mouths, teeth, smiles,
The tongues, the howls, the ferocities coming on and on
Were, you will tell me, his imagination –

But the tree he lay under, finished, staring, that was real,
A real hazel, and the pool it stood flourishing by, that pool
Was the crown knot of the thirteen unique waterfalls
Making and unmaking, deep, deep, always on the boil –

Not that he grasped it, all he grasped was he had come
To the end now, to a place there was no exit from
Up under thirteen falls which were too sheer to climb,
He was done for, let them tear him limb from limb,

He must sleep – And only when he slept and began to dream,
Only when he had given himself up did he begin to know
He had come where he would have said nobody ever came
Who was only as good or bad as he was – up the one stream

To the pool where angels met and gossiped before going down
Into the everyday world with their messages – Quite soon
Perhaps when he can't tell the dreams he has called his own
From the dreams in a hazel nut he will begin to feel

That the things he could not say or never dared to say
Are being said at last by the waters and by the angels getting away
With their good and bad news for people who live downstream
And he will not rejoice, nor will he grieve, he will stay

Where he is now, feeding the roots of an ever more beautiful hazel tree
By a pool in which waterfalls and angels come and go
And when at long last love's messenger, the hoopoe
Arrives with a message for him, only him, at the rendezvous

The hazel who has seen the angels staring at her wet in the sun
Dripping soft gold, flashing garnets, Bird, she will say,
That message for him from far far away and long long ago
He said we were one flesh, he and I, so just as well tell it me.

'Math and the Garden'

Rose Solari

Math and the Garden

It's all a matter of threes or fours,
like when my father died and it was
him and me and what he called god
and what I called whatever it was

that was next, only please not yet.
God won, which means that even if
he doesn't exist, He does. And Dad does
too, as river or beagle or five-year-old

prodigy writing his serious stanzas
in Latin. Which means, I guess,
that meaning is already here.
But I'm losing track. What I wanted

to say has something to do with
the dogwood, its four-petaled,
center-white blossoming that I want
every year to be more extravagant

than it is. As if the garden could be
compensation for some self-rising sap
that thins, the green seasonally less
insistent under the bud, despite all

that fertilizer and mulch. After the last
light rain in somebody's yard, the stars
disbelieving themselves, what I saw
on his face in that light was judgment

and then some. *Please*, I'd ask him.
Tell me again. I'm listening now.

'Passion killers'

Will May

Passion killers

Christ has finished his aria now, Dad.
This is where we come in. I've never had
such an off-key partner, your wayward hum
like an angry hoover. Our row has come
to flinch each time our copy lifts to bluff
your father's German, your voice enough
to turn Bach in his grave. But then there's me
whose birth prompted someone's vasectomy
and then troubled them to sleep on the floor,
making us both passion killers on that score.
Perhaps the tone deaf are past cure, and the
habitually estranged past caring.
The music would forgive us if it could
which, even if you don't believe, sounds good.

On the Mountain

Zoë Teale

(The opening of a novel, *On the Mountain*, which tells the story of a group of characters, and how they come together, as they climb Ben Nevis one midsummer day. The novel is largely set within a twenty-four hour period on the mountain's side.)

On the Mountain

Preface

There was something about the darkness in the valley that was not quite still. There was the usual rustle of small creatures, of leaves; the creaks and whining of the tree branches; the splutter of cold water chasing itself down the mountain toward the loch-side. But there was something else that did not fit. A small piece of the dark had broken loose and was moving slowly across the landscape, treading the mountain path. The stones shifted and split apart from one another, parting for the dark feet.

It was not morning for a long time. The lake was flat as a dead eye, reflecting the black sky, glinting occasionally as the clouds thinned to reveal a small half moon.

The figure stood watching over the lake and threw a shadow long across the still surface when the moon appeared. For an hour or more it stood. The night creatures read it as a thin rock, a standing stone peculiarly balanced. It quickly became a part of the landscape. But at last it decided that it would not stay.

The darkness began to withdraw, sucked into the black water. The bumps and lumps of the mountains and valley, the rocks and ridges, shook themselves free of the night and tilted it into the lake, so that the lake became blacker still and the air pale.

Against the white rock high up, the figure was moving slowly. It neared the top long before the new light day was shot with colour from the rising sun. It reached the summit as the first warm rays of orange and pink touched the bald head of the mountain.

The smallest hotel in Britain was sunk squat as a large grey rock on the top. Elsina saw him as he came in sight over the ridge. A man, wearing a suit and hat, but carrying no bags, which was unusual among those visiting.

Elsina watched him from the window at the end of the little room where she prepared breakfast. Only two visitors last night, and none tonight. The traveller could stay. She would find him something to change into, some spare vest of Mr Saxon's would do.

He had taken his hat off, and he was bald as the mountain on top. He was an ugly man, she thought. He had a tight little chin in a point, and now his hat was off she could see his huge ears sticking out either side of his head. Each man that came she looked at carefully. Hetty said she had more choice up here than any of them below, or more chance at any rate. But so many of them who came were married.

He turned his head. His skin was very pale. That was also unusual, because most were flushed as fired beetroot by the time they hauled themselves up here. There seemed to be no sweat on him. His lips were the only part that was red. And maybe his eyes.

Elsina put down her cloth and took the cold metal handle of the bucket.

'Just going to fetch the water,' she called. 'We've a customer already today and the sun's not risen.'

She could hear Mr Saxon grunting as he turned over.

As she walked out onto the summit the cold air stilled her for a moment. She called it the frozen moment. Every day it came, and although she had worked here for months, her body could not prepare for it, but each time shut in on itself to gather strength before opening again ready for another day.

And when she stepped forward, the man had gone. In that moment, as she opened the door, standing with her eyes and ears and limbs in shock at the biting air, in that frozen moment, as she said so often, for so many years after, until she was so old that she could not tell whether she had ever even climbed the mountain at all; in that frozen moment he had disappeared, and no one had ever found him, and most people did not even believe that he had ever existed.

Except there was the hat. A small black bowler hat, quite unsuited to life on the mountain, soft as a mole's fur and smelling very slightly of tobacco. On that morning Elsina had walked over to the hat and picked it up; it was still warm inside, as she tucked her hands in. She walked to the edge which she called God's Bite because since she had first seen it she thought the ridges on the cliff were like teeth marks in a huge chunk of cheese and she liked imagining God taking bites out of his earth to make it the right shape. But she did not think about that as she stood cradling the hat. She looked for the man in black but there was no sign of him and no sound.

She looked back at the little stone hut, settled firmly as though it had grown out of the mountain. Then she returned to the bucket.

The ice was thick. It was always thick. But that morning Elsina's hands broke it easily and she didn't feel the cold. She dipped the bucket in. Her nose was running and she could not wipe it. Slowly she walked in the mountain silence back toward the hut, folding the hat in the plentiful rough material of her skirts. As she pushed open the little door and returned to the warmth, the cold bucket banged at her leg. Her arm was shaking.

'What's up with you?' Mr Saxon said in his usual grim way. And then his voice softened a little. 'Hey, Elsie. What's up? You look like you've seen a ghost.' And he took the bucket, handing her a white handkerchief.

*

She did not say anything to anyone about the man at first, and when at last she did, and search parties were sent looking for a body, he was not found. Guests came and went as usual. There was an artist who stayed in order to paint the clouds and the peaks in differing weathers and Elsina throughout her life remembered how he liked his egg, and how on his last morning the sun shone bright through a hole in the clouds, as if God was peaking through. She watched him retreating down the mountain path until he was no bigger than the stones that he walked on.

Two souvenirs she kept of her time working on the mountain. An artist's brush and a gentleman's black hat.

*

Years later Elsina returned from Edinburgh with her three children to start life again at the foot of the mountain. Her husband had died in a factory in Leith and she was given a small amount of money to compensate for the loss of him. There were many tourists at this time and she decided to set up a little cake and sweet shop for the visitors, with her nearly grown children helping out with the baking and taking of orders. Elsina did very well with her business. She ended up buying a comfortable house in the centre of town, and her children all married well, though only one, Maria, stayed close by, marrying a doctor and becoming quite a pillar of society.

Maria had two children, born in 1916 and 1918, little war babies, and Elsina lived long enough to see these two grow up, dying just before the outbreak of the next war. She gave her most treasured possessions to her grand-daughter Ellen, and among these were her wedding ring, an old paint brush with a red ribbon tied about it, and a worn black hat. Ellen, who never married, passed her grandmother's box of oddments to the town's museum shortly before her death at the age of eighty-nine.

The curator of the museum was called Jane Scarr. Even the dullest of things were brought to life by her skill at creating a history for some object or other out of more or less thin air. She was thrilled with Elsina's box, and even more so when unpacking the hat she noticed a stiffness in the brim of it, as if something had been stitched inside. Very carefully, with a small Stanley knife, she slit the old stitches and drew out from the pouch a piece of paper folded into a narrow strip. It was a letter, and the hat with its missive beside it became the central piece in a new 'Millennium' cabinet of finds from the mountain's sides.

It read:

Dear —

I have nowhere to send this letter to, no address. I send it voyaging into the future as one day no doubt people like us will be sent off toward the stars. Who knows who this will reach, and what your world will be.

My aim is very simple. I am in love and my love will be nothing. She is governess at the castle – was, for a week since she left for London with our baby deep within her not yet visible to anyone. She has decided against me, having decided for me many times as we walked together, imagining Keats's walking here and more.

My wish, to be clear – that this one day reaches my son or daughter if indeed that you be.

That you know how your father loved you; that his name was Peter Fox. That he was cursed with the ugliest looks a man could have, but was once thought beautiful inside.

I think it is a curse, for I believe my father did as I will do, perhaps even my grandfather about whom no one ever spoke to me. The women used to talk of some wrong, that made for unhappiness in life and was only to be lifted by one who climbs and jumps but has no limbs to climb and jump – some such, my mother said. I hear the three witches, and yet I have not the energy or desire to work the riddle.

I hope to God the looks and the leaps have run their course with you. I am able to do no more than pray this reaches you, and I will love eternally my Sarah – Sarah Ericsson – my Viking Sarah, who took the only good of me and nurtured it a while, and turned it to the joint-root of her seed.

My wishes to the future.
Peter Fox

Jane Scarr had tried to find a relation of this man, in vain. There were no Foxes at all, except in the graveyard, and her interest had now waned. There were always so many other threads to follow in the labyrinthine paths of local past, so many photos that could not be placed, and faces that could not be named.

People came and read the sorry message. One or two pondered whether it might have been a relative of their own.

But on 20th June 200-, the day before midsummer, a woman arrived in Fort William with a postcard in her handbag written in the same hand.

Zulu Speaking

Elleke Boehmer

Zulu Speaking

The lock was asking for trouble. Grace had meant to mention it to her boss Mr Rodgers from the day she had come to work here as an assistant secretary, almost exactly six months ago. It had sat there staring at her, five metres in front of her nose, shiny with over-use, soft to the touch, and she had done nothing about it. She had kept meaning to, but then something would come up, a phone call, a diary clash, an urgent order, and the thought to take action would disappear from her mind.

The thing was, the import-export trade in the country these days was busy, buzzing you could say, due to how it was based in the old-fashioned barter on which most parties in the world's developing countries had the low-down. At times, when the exchange rate was especially jumpy and all over the place, the business grew frantic. Grace processed up to twenty, twenty-five deliveries a day. There wasn't the time to make sure to carry out practical chores.

Most nights, she worked late and caught up on her sleep at the weekends, which didn't impress sports-mad Charley, who liked to have his wife support him in his golf tournaments and rugby games. Eight in the morning to six in the evening and sometimes later, the office phone never stopped ringing. Faxes with Chinese letterheads spat out from the fax machine. China, in particular, was keen on the raw materials of a free South Africa, fruit and metals mainly, swapped at a favourable rate for light-bulbs, yoga mats, kids' toys, plastic kitchen-ware and tableware, including cheap melamine coasters and bread-boards, also stationery items, brightly coloured plastic sandals, candles scented and unscented, even car parts – and the thousand other products that they, China, were happy to give in exchange.

Still, despite the frantic activity, Grace would sit on the phone here in the small reception room, at the big chipped 1950s desk, the column of drawers on either side of her chair, with the phone pressed to her shoulder, and she would see the lock taunting her. I'm trouble, it said, do something about me, that single Yale lock that was so worn the key slid into it like a hot knife through butter, and this on a door leading off from the street. Their office was located in one of the converted settler bungalows with thick stone walls and iron lattice details around the frontage, that still filled the Central Business District, even after the two new office buildings with their three floors of parking garages had sprung up on Church Street. A visitor stepped straight from the narrow earthen front porch, polished colonial red, into Grace's office. There was no parking whatsoever connected to the bungalow. Grace took the bus into work.

Mr Rodgers of course had made sure to stick a laminated sign on the door saying no money was housed on the premises overnight. In the import-export sector, it stood to reason, petty cash is kept to a minimum. But who could guarantee that thieves could read, and, even if they could, opportunists that they were, that they gave themselves the time to notice the warning when jimmying the door and forcing their way in? And what might lead them to believe such a notice anyway? A white-owned business would surely have money sitting about somewhere, even if not in ready-to-hand cash form. That, too, stood to reason.

In the event – in *the* event – the thieves came during business hours, just as if soliciting for work, the tried-and-tested method. It was the start of the week, Monday, a relatively easy day, when you're less on your mettle than on hectic Thursdays and Fridays – though Fridays, Grace knew, could be quiet in some trading-partner countries, because of Muslim prayers. Her secretary friends had warned her of intruders' favourite tricks like this one, the knock at the door half-way through the morning, but when the moment came, did she remember? Did she hear warning bells? You're too laid-back, Grace, too relaxed, they often said, and rightly so, you trust too much. One day, you'll come a-cropper.

Grace at the time was filing her nails (she was ashamed when she had to mention this in the crime report). She was filing her nails, and gazing away at the only poster she had on the wall, a Kwazulu-Natal Tour Board poster, of the Amphitheatre on a flawless blue-sky day. It was unusual to be doing this, day-dreaming basically, she added in her crime report statement. But the fax machine this morning had stayed silent. Mr Rodgers was at a morning meeting in Durban together with Jane, his PA. The only other person about was Samson, their all-purposes man, messenger, fixer, cleaner, pottering somewhere in the office backyard. He heard not a thing of the event, it was that quick. Silent but violent, you might say, if you were minded to make light of it. Over in an instant.

So she was taking the opportunity of the quiet time to neaten her nails while thinking about holidays, where they might go for their winter break this year, about how the Amphitheatre National Park had been their honeymoon destination only two years back and had looked perfect, exactly as pictured. She was at that very moment finishing her second hand, her left, leaning back a little to admire her work. Generally, she was thinking, she preferred to take a short break close to home, the province alone had so much of beauty. True, the names of distant lands on the letters she daily received were beginning to tempt her fancy, but she had to take into account that exotic locations left Charley cold. He wanted to be assured – no, guaranteed – there would be at least a nine-hole golf course close to wherever they went on holiday, and in some countries the availability of such facilities wasn't always easy to ascertain.

The old Yale lock at the time was on, naturally. Around the centre of town none of the offices in converted houses that led off the pavement kept an open door. The men even knocked, a few sharp raps, nothing out of the ordinary, as if they were legitimate visitors. Grace took a moment to put the nail file back in the top drawer where she kept it, the top drawer on the right, and walked over to the door. The distance was just a few steps.

A quick check through the spy-hole revealed nothing unusual. Two Africans, and a third, she soon found out, hidden behind the first two, a short man, hardly man-sized, with a leg shrivelled by polio. He was the one who ended up keeping lookout at the door. She only ever saw his feet, his one normal black patent shoe and his tiny built-up shoe like a kid's, very scuffed but real leather.

It was when she laid eyes on their clothes, though difficult to spot through the spy-hole, that she felt the first tweak of alarm. The clothes were suspiciously new, the folds still sharp in the shirts. But by now it was too late. Her hand was on the Yale, and the snib slid back smoothly. The door was coming open and they had entered, in single file, the first man indoors raising his hand, as if doffing a non-existent hat, for an instant almost like a gentlemen.

Then, suddenly, dropping the politeness, the 'morning mem' and 'how are you?', one of the men, the one who came in second, grabbed her shoulders and fell to the floor on top of her. She heard something crack and bounce and only later worked out from the bruise and the lump that it must have been the sound of her own skull-bone, the back of her head, hitting the floor.

The first man meanwhile kicked the outside door closed, the Yale obligingly clicking into place, and swooped over to her desk, playing aeroplanes like a boy, she thought at the time, his arms stretched out as if to grab everything off its top. His very pale pink palms spread wide were the last things she saw. The pain of the fall suddenly jolted through her head, a delayed reaction, and her eyes shut tight. She kept them closed and let her body slump. There was no need to make a conscious decision. Never put up a fight, they said at physical defense classes, but fear had already turned her body to pulp.

Not rape, was her thought, feeling the man's knee on her ribs, please, not rape, and then, when there was something cold against her throat, God, no, not stabbing. Her thoughts now shrank to nothing but basic, clinical functions, as if her brain was in hypothermia, she later thought, the organ carrying out no more than what was required to live.

She registered that it was the end of the month, of course, of course. Why hadn't she realized this at the door, when the lock was still safely on? These guys wanted money, payment, if only for their outlay, their smart clothes, the polished shoes she had seen gleaming as they entered.

She heard music burst from a passing car out in the street, Neil Diamond's 'Hot August Night'. But it's July, she said to herself inconsequentially. It's July and it's chilly and out there in the street everyone is carrying on as normal.

Then she began to feel the growing pain in her chest, under the second man's pressing knee, and the darting stabs of discomfort, also increasing in force, at the back of her head. She squeezed her eyes tighter shut. Please, please, not rape, she thought again, and wondered to whom she was addressing this unspoken plea. This cold at her neck, was it a knife or a gun? Seeing as he'd gone so far as to bring along a weapon, wouldn't the man set about using it at some point soon?

She heard the first man put his shoulder to the door leading to Mr Rodgers's office, closed but not locked, thank goodness, which would minimize damage, she registered even at the time, lying there. She heard the two men talking amongst themselves, the second man only inches above her face, their voices very low and quick, speaking Zulu but with English words mixed in, *cash box*, *alarm*, *alarm*? *cell*, *fax*, her *cell*, where was it? the *filing cabinet*? They seemed to know enough office vocabulary to get by. There was some reference to her, lying there like a dead cow, they said, harmless like a dead cow. And no one else was about, they added, gloating audibly, just as they'd hoped.

They've talked this all through in advance, Grace realized, rolling the back of her head on the floor just slightly, to ease the discomfort. They've put in the planning, they've exercised forethought. Definitely, they must be proper thieves. They'd the whole job worked out in advance. Early to say, but maybe, just maybe, they did theft instead of doing rape. Maybe they were professional thieves, no more than just proper thieves, inconveniencing people, but not blasting their lives. Then again, thieves did murder, if they had to, and sometimes even if not. Sometimes killing happened as collateral damage, the papers said so every day.

The second man's hands, she could feel, were busy with her neck and arms, her top half only, pressing the knife to her skin, she thought not a gun, no, the instrument was too slim. His hand wrenched her gold chain, a twenty-first birthday present from her parents, off her neck. Again, she felt no immediate pain, though the wrenching drew blood. She felt the wetness of it on her skin. As the man yanked she wanted to reach out, grab the chain back, but her neatly filed hands, one lying under her back, the other clamped somehow against the man's warm, cotton-shirted side, did nothing.

And now, a pull at her arm. She was rolled onto her side. She was sure she didn't open her eyes, maybe just glanced through the film of her lashes. Her wrists were being tied with a bit of muddy skipping rope, she found when they'd left, a leftover from some previous job no doubt, involving a household with kids. She was being pushed and pulled, dragged like some dead cow, yes, exactly, or sack of potatoes, towards her own desk, round to the back of it, her own side, the space where her legs went.

Hamba, hamba. Go, go, said the man, his only words to her so far, his shoe against her bottom, shoving. The kick hurt, but the words stilled something in her, softened something, she didn't know how.

Eyes shut, she crawled in under the desk as far as she could go, till her forehead touched the wooden panel she sometimes rested her feet against. He shoved her again, using a kind of kick, what felt like a heave of his foot into the small of her back, and barked in rough English, 'Where the petty cash? Say, say. Say, not show.'

But her lips wouldn't move. One side of her mouth felt loose and foolish, as if she'd had a local anaesthetic at the dentist's. She tried to shift an arm. The skipping rope pulled at her wrists. She wanted to press a hand to her lips, to get them to work. The man made a hoicking sound, a yerch of disgust. She'd been too slow. She heard him smash something into one of the desk drawers, probably the instrument that had been at her neck. But the drawer gave no trouble. The petty cash-box rattled as he pulled it out and placed it on the desk above her head.

The cash-box was the first of a string of items the men now seemed to be lining up on her desk. There was Mr Rodgers's radio, she gauged from their one-word remarks, and her cell phone, lying there anyway, and the fax machine, and Mr Rodgers's PC and printer. Her PC was already in place for them. 'Bag, hand-bag,' the second man muttered, even as she, peeping, saw her bag elevate itself from where it had been standing under her chair. Her purse was pulled out, she heard the familiar rasp of the sequin decoration on the side as it scraped against the zipper opening of the bag. Her bag descended back down, this time to the seat of the chair.

Meanwhile from Mr Rodgers's room came the intermittent sound of crashing and banging, as if the first man were dismantling the filing cabinet, or pulling out the drawers, making sure nothing worth having was left behind. Maybe he was trying to find something, shopping bags, cardboard boxes, to assist with carrying out the stuff. Feet began to thump the floor, to and fro, to and fro, from Mr Rodgers's room past the desk to the front. They were getting the stuff out now, Grace thought to herself, they had to be, it had been a while, they were piling it at the front door in readiness, they would be on their way.

She tried to adjust the position of her left leg, which was folded under her right and had gone to sleep. But she moved jerkily and ended up bumping the desk, rattling nerves overhead. Again came the kick, the heave to the small of her back, almost right up her bum this time. The kick didn't hurt as much as the first one, but the shove forwards thudded the bruised place on her skull against the desk. A strange sound, like a strangulated yawn, came from her.

'The cow's groaning,' said one of the men, probably the first, with what sounded like a sneer. 'The cow is only half-dead.'

He thinks nothing of me, the awareness sliced through Grace, but the thought aroused no particular reaction. Of course he'd be indifferent, it made sense. Hadn't she been as inanimate as possible? And, indifferent was good. Far worse would have been if she'd been an obstacle to them, inciting their anger. God knows what would have happened then. Besides, calling her a dead cow, she knew, the men weren't intending to insult her. They didn't mean for her to follow them. She wasn't meant to get their meaning.

They don't know I understand their language, she thought to herself, they think their conversation slips me by. She was white, English-speaking, in her twenties, she'd been to school in the old system – so how would she get Zulu? How in the world could she be Zulu-speaking?

And then, suddenly, it dawned on her – yes, that she *understood* them. She had followed them, not only their every word but also the expression in their voices, the whispers, the significant pauses. Though she hadn't meant to, hadn't even consciously realized it, even as their words stilled her, she'd picked up their Zulu along with their English, from the start.

At her high school down in Durban, after all, no one had taught Zulu. The image of Florence's quick, bright look came like a balm to Grace's tightly shut eyes. Even if Zulu had been offered at her school, she remembered, her parents would have insisted she not take it. Why clog the brain with Zulu when there are important world languages, gateways to great civilizations, to be learned? Zulu was for rough white boys who'd grown up on farms, though most took pains to forget it as soon as they came down to boarding school in the city.

But Florence, short, spry, fast-moving, very dark, the 'laundry girl' for their entire street, she had taught Grace Zulu regardless. Florence had trained as a teacher, but missed the final diploma exam because, she once explained in a hurry, uncharacteristically swallowing her words, her father had died and the family's funds had run out. In the laundry room, nothing bothered, she turned her attentions to Grace. When she and Grace were alone together, Florence used Zulu for everything.

But it was only because she, Florence, was persistent, and Grace admired her, how quickly she moved, how readily she laughed, how her eyes missed nothing, it was only because of the bond they had, that the Zulu words she taught stuck. Grace the teenager was a dedicated resident of North Beach, then called a banana girl, who liked to cultivate a blank look, a relaxed, loping walk like a boy's, and lemon-juice bleached hair. Grace the banana girl was devoted to swimming and sun-bathing, not to learning.

Florence sniffed at her look, her slack walk, at how she lay in the sun and basted her skin in sunflower oil.

'You want to be brown as me, Grace? Why? I own nothing. In this society I count for nothing. I'm not even a teacher. You must get off your bottom. You've got to learn things to get by in this world, even if you're whiter than banana fruit inside.'

'You count for something, Florence, 'course you do,' Grace said in return, every time. 'You're Zulu. Zulu is special, you say so yourself.'

'Then learn your Zulu, Grace, learn it. Tell me, what is the word for, let's see, banana? *Banana girl?*'

And so today, crouched under her own desk with her wrists tied, Grace got the men's meaning, even when they talked low and quick. Florence had taught her well. *Go, go*, they were saying to one another now, urgently, *Hamba, Hamba*. They were at the end of the job. The door was at last opened, then shut again. The obliging Yale lock barely clicked. The lookout seemed to have departed and the other two were waiting for him. She heard their breathing.

It was time for her to speak, now or never.

'*Ngiyacela, ngingayithola imali yebhasi elizongisa ekhaya na?* Please,' she added in English for good measure, 'Can I have my bus-fare home?'

'Hau?' said the first man, '*Uthini umfazi?*' What is the woman saying?

'*Uyasikhuluma isiZulu. Uyasikhuluma isiZulu.*' She is speaking Zulu to us, said the second man, she is definitely speaking Zulu.

Silence, then a scuffling. '*Dlula. Dlula.*' Go on. A hand slapped down on another hand. There was the sound of money, a few coins, enough, the fare and a rand or so extra, rattling down on the desk overhead. They confirmed it for her. Even before they'd spoken she predicted the words they'd use.

'*Ishiye etafuleni imali yakhe yebhasi elizomusa ekhaya.*'

As familiar as if Florence had spoken them. Leave the bus-fare on the table, said for her benefit.

Afterwards, when free victim-support counselling was offered, Grace didn't sign up. Charley tried to persuade her to accept, but every time she agreed to his request, she didn't get round to making the booking. Even to herself she didn't go into her reasons why.

She had the nightmares about the burglary she was expected to have, but they weren't too bad, mainly she dreamed she was being kicked and shoved about, and after a while the dreams passed. For a number of months she suffered embarrassing yawning fits whenever she passed a group of young black men in the street. But these too passed, as she'd read they would.

Immediately following the break-in Mr Rodgers gave her a fortnight's leave with pay, to which she added her winter holiday week, and she and

Charley enjoyed a long break in Wilderness, in a hotel next to an 18-hole golf-course. In Wilderness there wasn't the temptation to listen into Zulu conversations. Most people in the area spoke either Xhosa or English.

When she returned to work, Mr Rodgers had fitted a double Chubb lock to the door, and installed a thief-proof intercom system, which helped her enormously in getting back to her relaxed but efficient office-girl self.

She knew she had got off the whole thing lightly, had got *over* it lightly, too, and she knew why this was so. This fact of this *lightly*, she suspected, explained her reluctance to seek counseling. It certainly explained why she didn't want to talk about the experience. She didn't want to say the words, I got off lightly. I got off with only a bad bruise on my head and a few bad dreams and I think I know why. She didn't want to say, well, it wasn't exactly prisoner's syndrome, but early on in the experience I began to grasp what the thieves were after, you could say I somehow followed my captor's meaning. Or not just *somehow*. I know how. It's this unlikely thing, I speak Zulu, not too badly. I know the language. I'm a Zulu-speaking banana girl. Something connected me to those thieves, in spite of myself. And by the end they knew it, too. They acknowledged it.

The single change in her life was that she developed a secret liking for the radio. Switched back on to her memories of Florence, of the laundry room and learning Zulu, she made excuses to stay at home on Saturday afternoons instead of going with Charley to the golf club. Since the break-in she'd begun to suffer from occasional headaches, nothing to worry about, though irksome, so her excuses weren't always just white lies.

Still, headache or no, it became her favourite thing to stay at home on Saturday afternoons. No sooner had Charley driven off than she would make a cup of tea, organic rooibos had been Florence's favourite. She would sit in the comfortable armchair with her eyes shut, her legs stretched out, and listen to the Zulu plays that were broadcast on Saturday afternoons on the radio.

The Bloomers

Manish Chauhan

(Extract from a novel)

The Bloomers

Chapter One, Winter

Dressed in her husband's pyjamas, Radha Shukla brought down the sink with a hammer. She then proceeded to heap the broken cupboards and chairs into the centre of the shop floor and brought out a large bucket filled with water. Getting down on her knees she scrubbed the dark wood using a scrubber too old for the task. Coming across a difficult patch she pushed harder, the dark grain refusing to shed its mark until the scrubbing took control of her and she stood up, throwing the thing across the room and breaking a window.

Only then did she begin to cry – each sob heavier than the previous, dark pools of water emerging from the pit of her stomach. She felt like an overflowing vessel and finally the floor had come undone beneath her. She fell to her knees. If her children could see her now! Crying like a mad woman in the middle of her empty shop. And despite this she continued, her tears falling harder and faster with each breath, her body shaking uncontrollably and her nose running as she pressed her palms firmly against the floor.

After it was done, she sat on a stool and eased her hiccups. Was it that she was alone? Or was it that everything suddenly appeared to be so new? Now that he was gone, everything frightened her – most of all that she was too old for this. Too old to be starting again. If he were still alive, things would be different.

As she looked up, however, she was stunned that he was standing four feet in front of her. He had seen her crying. How would she explain herself? And his pyjamas, how would she explain those? It had to be her imagination, the tears blurring her vision but, no, he was still there when she wiped her eyes, got up from her stool and walked towards him.

'What's all of this?' he asked, in his familiar disapproving tone and her heart sank. Suddenly conscious of her dishevelled hair, her wet face and the existence of the shop in which she was stood, Radha covered her face.

'Is it you?' she wanted to ask, but of course it was him. He was there, in those horrible brown trousers he refused to throw out. That was him, stubborn as ever, standing there, watching her gulp for air. And, there, in that moment, she felt embarrassed.

Unsure of what to do, she turned away from him and ran her hands over the loose hair that strayed from her bun. It was then that a strange thought occurred to Radha. Had he ever seen her completely naked? Even during the course of their marriage? Maybe a breast, she considered, but never everything in its entirety. And they had always had sex under the darkness of a light switched off and the heaviness of a quilt. Other than those few occasions she had spent most of her life sleeping in a bed gown.

She felt uncomfortable, as though the veil she had held so closely around herself for forty-six years was slowly slipping. Slipping and falling. There she was: Radha Shukla, recent widow, aspiring businesswoman, mother, lady who sobbed like a mad woman. There she was. Her dead husband standing watching her.

'I don't know why you're crying,' he said. 'You're finally free.'

'Shut up! Shut up!' she said trying to hold back any further tears. 'You've gone.'

'You couldn't even look at me,' he said, clenching his fist. 'You wanted me out of your life more than anything.'

'Stop it, stop it,' she cried, and she was seized by her sobs once again, the sound rising and falling, increasing frantically until she felt the urge to shake him. Of course, by the time she turned to confront him, he had gone, and she had no idea where.

Two hours later the heap of rubbish grew to its fullest and Radha looked at it, a bonfire waiting for the flame. She took a broom and gathered the dust from the surrounding floor, moving it into one corner. It had taken her the entire day but finally the shop was ready for the plasterers. It was only then that she walked towards the broken window and reached for the larger pieces of glass that lay scattered in the street. She looked out onto the main road, the slow ripples of winter smoke moving steadily along the uneven sky. Clusters of dead leaves moving from one end of the road to the other and over the cars that made their way home in the rush hour.

She fetched a roll of tape and some pieces of cardboard with which she attempted to board up the window when she saw Maya approach from the side of the shop. Radha noticed that her daughter had tied her hair using one of her old floral headscarves. She was reminded of herself those years ago when she had wrapped the scarf tightly around her head before leaving the house. Her daughter wore it like a bandana.

'Mum, what are you doing?' asked Maya, dropping the bags she was carrying to the floor and rushing over to help.

'Why do you tie your hair like that?' asked Radha. 'And where did you get that scarf?'

'Oh god, I just got here! Here, give it to me.' Maya took one side of the board, pushing it carefully into the corner of the window frame.

'It makes you look like a hippy. Is that what you want people to think? And the skirt…' Radha stopped, motioning for her to go outside.

'What about it?'

'It's unusual, weird, with the frill in that place. Is it new?'

'It's vintage,' said Maya, exasperated, as she looked over her mother's outfit.

'Why can't you dress like other girls?'

'Who did this?' Maya asked, changing the subject.

'I just put the broom against the window before I lifted those chairs,' Radha answered. 'It must have landed hard.' She dragged the large roll of tape across the board and secured it.

'You should have been more careful. What if somebody breaks in during the night?'

'If they want to break in let them. What is there to take anyway?'

'Have you been crying?' Maya noticed the pale red surrounding her mother's eyes.

'No. I was thinking about your father. That's all.'

'You did a good job. The skip will be here tomorrow to take everything away.'

'Take everything away,' Radha repeated, looking around the shop, aware of its emptiness and staring into the pile of broken wood in the centre. And then at the walls, without any colour.

*

Later that evening, once they had returned home, Radha lit the fire in the living room and sat beside the flames for a short while. She closed her eyes momentarily as the heat made its way from her hands to her face and over her head.

From the corner of the room she saw the flash of a red light on the telephone pad. Ravi.

'You don't have to cook, I'll do it,' she then shouted from the living room, as Maya went about preparing their dinner.

Since her father's death, Maya prepared more and more of their meals, asking her mother only when unsure of where in the kitchen certain ingredients were kept. To Radha's surprise, she found her daughter's cooking edible.

Taking two small onions from the vegetable basket, Maya began to peel each slowly, the papery skin slipping between her fingers and tumbling into the sink.

Radha came and stood behind her.

'Can you get the chillies and the *dhana*?'

Radha walked to the fridge and brought out three plastic bags. Placing the various ingredients onto the work surface she began to pull the stalk from the top of each chilli and the stems from the end of the coriander. The leaves scattered over the work surface like green flakes of snow.

'Did he send you a message?' Radha asked suddenly, as though they were resuming an entirely different conversation. It had occurred to her that she had given Maya's telephone number to Kusum Joshi who had wanted it for her son.

'Not yet.' Maya pulled out a saucepan from inside the kitchen cabinet and drizzled some oil into it before turning on the heat and frying off the onions. Radha switched on the extractor fan.

'Two days,' Radha thought aloud. 'He should have sent you a message by now. Kusum went out of her way to ask me for your number.'

'It doesn't matter,' Maya concluded and emptied some pressure-cooked *mugh* into the onions before adding the crushed ginger and sliced chillies. She noticed her mother's eyes on her. This wasn't her mother's method of cooking *mugh* but her own, or rather, Madhur Jaffrey's.

As the yellow *daal* began to simmer, Radha retrieved the big bowl and began to bind the dough for the *rotli*.

Taking a small piece of *atta* Maya formed a ball, pressed it down firmly onto the *patlo* and rolled it out into a small circle.

'You know, when we were young...' said Radha. She placed the chapattis under the grill. 'I'm talking about a time even before I got married. Whenever a boy's family came to view a girl, his mother would check that her *rotli* were round and that she could cook a *papad* on the flames without burning it or herself. They say that if your *rotli* are round, it means that you'll find a good husband.'

'I better get a plate out then and cut around it.'

After a while mother and daughter sat down to their meal – *daal*, *rotlis*, *anthanoo*, *papad*, a spoonful each of yesterday's left over *bhinda*.

'I had a call from Veena Aunty yesterday,' Radha said. 'Her nephew has returned from Japan. He works for a big company.'

'Uh huh.' Maya knew precisely where the conversation was leading and concentrated on her meal in an attempt to avoid her mother's gaze. Lately she had been regretting asking her mother to point out suitable boys within their *Saamaj*. She recalled the conversation she had with Nina during their yoga class that morning.

'I can't believe you've asked your mother to do that already. You're 24!' Nina said, as she went from the cat *asana* into a dog.

'But I'm having no luck with guys. I've dated so many pricks it's time for a change. Would it really be so bad to meet some guys who were within the *Saamaj*? It saves so much time and trouble. You know where you are from day one.'

'Within the *Saamaj*? God, you sound like my mum. Look, I don't know about you, but the men in my *Saamaj* are ugly as hell and complete mummy's boys.'

Maya saw that Nina said the word complete with her head titled back, her lips wide and her eyes slightly bulging, the same way she might say the word 'disgusting'.

'I guess I'm surprised that you're taking this so seriously. Isn't there anything you want to do before you get married?'

And Maya heard the concern in her voice that had been sitting quietly behind the outrage.

'Of course there is.' Maya tried to balance her body carefully before falling flatly onto her yoga mat. The instructor, Nilima Devi, gave her a stern look. Maya mouthed an apology and repositioned herself.

'There are so many things I want to do, but wouldn't it be good to be able to do them with your husband?'

'Marriage is the last thing on my mind, and you should warn your mother not to spend too much time speaking with mine. I don't want her getting ideas.'

In the six weeks since she had first asked her mother to point out eligible bachelors, Radha had arranged four meetings. Maya got the distinct feeling that her mother enjoyed arranging these regardless of the fact that she now had a new shop to attend to. This probably stemmed from the fact that she had never had any such opportunity with her elder sister Seema.

'Why don't you send him a message? I have this number.' Radha looked up at Maya who was finishing the last of her meal. 'Meet him once and twice, see if you get along, no problem in that is there?'

The thought occurred to Radha, in a small flash, that soon she would be alone. Her children would all have left her and then what?

'Look, give me his number but I'm not promising anything,' Maya said. She gathered the plates and took them into the kitchen.

*

As Maya went about the washing, Radha listened to the messages left on her answer machine. Ravi had called some three hours ago. She pressed the call back button and listened to the ring.

'Hi. What are you doing?' he asked, when he answered. Radha could hear music in the background – the bashing of drums that she herself detested but which her son seemed to love. Banging drums and screaming boys she called it. He said it was Metallica.

'Where are you?'

'At a party.'

'Did you eat?'

'Yeah'

'What?'

'Pizza?'

'Again? How many pizzas in one week? Why don't you cook using all of those *masala* I packed for you? I taught you so many dishes before you left.' And then, 'Too much cheese can cause headaches. I read it in the paper. It can even cause blocked arteries.'

'Listen, Mum, can I call you tomorrow? I need to go.'

'Where?'

'To the party.'

'Oh.' What could she do to keep him on the phone? She looked up at the ceiling briefly. Nothing. At least he was with other people and not alone. 'Call me tomorrow and don't forget, I'll wait for you.' She knew he would call, he always called. But she threatened him regardless. This was her way of telling Ravi that she missed him more than she had missed the girls. That secretly within herself she could no longer bear the thought of spending her entire life alone. And so she threatened to cut his allowance if he didn't telephone her daily. And it had worked so far.

*

Later that night, after Radha had fallen asleep, Maya went into her bedroom, sat on the edge of her bed and rolled herself a joint. She untied the scarf from her head and ran her hands through her curls before removing her make-up in front of the mirror. Opening the bedroom window she lit the joint and concentrated on the thin layers of heady smoke that drew patterns in the sky. She reached for her mobile phone and proceeded to type a text message to Jiten Joshi. She hadn't felt it necessary to tell her mother that the boy had contacted her as soon as he received her number. They had arranged to meet for a drink the following day.

She considered whether she should also send a message to the latest on her mother's list of bachelors, Arun Bhatt.

Hi Arun, this is Maya Shukla. My Mum gave me your number. How r u? Hpe ur well.

Shortly after, she brushed her teeth, lay on her bed and opened the novel she was reading when she was distracted by the gentle flash of her telephone screen.

Hi Maya. Gd to hr frm u. Hw r u dng? I'm gd thanx. This is slightly weird isnt it?

Thinking carefully before she responded, Maya tried to imagine what Arun looked like but she wasn't certain.

Yes this is weird. But it wld be btr to tlk over a drnk smtime if ur free? Hw abt nxt wk?

Tht's a gd idea. Which dts r u available?

Each time Maya arranged another meeting she found herself acutely aware of how unromantic it all was. No mild flirtation, no deep pangs of longing the way it had been with her previous boyfriends. But that would come, she assured herself. That would come.

One of those Days

Mark Burton

ONE OF THOSE DAYS

POST PRODUCTION SCRIPT

FADE IN...

A medley of indistinct voices, some foreign, some barking
through megaphones. Over the buzz, a young man's voice, a
man clearly under a strain.

> STEWARD 1
> ... yeah look we're all having a bad
> day okay? So just try and be patient,
> please...

EXT. BLEAK LANDSCAPE. DAY.

CLOSE UP on crowds of people shuffling wearily past the
camera. They're being supervised by harassed stewards with
fluorescent yellow jackets and megaphones.

> STEWARDS
> Stay behind the barricades... one
> queue, please, just one queue...

> STEWARD 2
> (o.s, on megaphone)
> We do apologise for the wait... but be
> assured that everyone will be seen in
> due course...

The queue is restless, uneasy. As the music rises to a
crescendo we cut wide to reveal that it's NO ORDINARY
QUEUE. It stretches for mile after mile into a bleak and
blasted horizon framed by an imposing office building.

A manic-looking BLINDMAN is intoning to anyone who will
listen.

                    BLINDMAN
        Repent ye of ye sins, for this day all
        shall be judged in the eyes of the
        Lord!

The crowd hustles forward, past a CHEAP SIGN nailed to a
stake which features an arrow and the words: "JUDGEMENT DAY
(INDOORS IF WET)"

We now see all the stewards have ANGEL written in luminous
letters on their back. Stressed voices bark over their
walkie-talkies.

                    STEWARD 3
                (On Walkie Talkie)
        We're going to have to cut some
        corners guys -- what about sending all
        the timeshare reps straight down?
                (radio squawk)

                    VOICE ON WALKIE TALKIE
        We're already doing that Mike.

The stewards look round at the crowds, shaking their heads.

                    STEWARD 4
        This is so crap.

                    STEWARD 5
        Yeah man, the whole concept's wrong.
        It should be called 'judgement week' --
        or 'judgement year.'

                    STEWARD 6
        It's totally messed up...

DISSOLVE TO

INT. JUDGEMENT DAY OFFICE. DAY.

A neat but overcrowded reception area. It could be the
Passport Office.

TITLE CARD: ONE OF THOSE DAYS

We pick up with some First World War German soldiers as
they push their way aggressively through the orderly queue,
barging past a LATE-MIDDLE-AGED MAN.

> HOWARD
> Hey, hey! Stop pushing in! Fucking
> Germans...

> JEAN
> Howard!

> HOWARD
> Well.

He notices Jean looking nervously at an information stand
featuring various leaflets and forms about sins and
sinning. He snaps his newspaper and folds it neatly away.

> HOWARD (CONT'D)
> Look Jean, we've led completely
> blameless lives. We've never done
> anything remotely sinful...
> (bit wistful)
> anything.

> JEAN
> (equally wistful)
> No...

> PLEASANT PRE-RECORDED VOICE
> "Judgement counter number 3 please!

> JEAN
> ...that's us...

Jean nudges Howard. As they walk over to the counter she
catches her breath, checks her hair.

> HOWARD
> Relax.

The young counter clerk is keen and pleasant as he opens
their file.

>   COUNTER CLERK
>   Hello. Sorry about the wait --
>   it's just, er, crazy today... suppose
>   we should've seen it coming really...

They all give a slightly forced laugh.

>   COUNTER CLERK (CONT'D)
>   Now then, regarding your application
>   to join the Kingdom of Heaven and sit
>   at the foot of our Lord...
>   (he flicks through)
>   Yup, should be pretty
>   straightforward...

Howard and Jean give each other a faint smile.

>   COUNTER CLERK (CONT'D)
>   Yeah, don't think there's any real
>   problems...
>   (turns a page; puzzled
>   expression)
>   Ah! Umm...

>   HOWARD
>   Is everything alright?

>   COUNTER CLERK
>   It's nothing. Just give me a second.

He goes over to a smartly-dressed supervisor and shows her
the file. The supervisor looks across, nodding. Presently,
the clerk returns.

>   COUNTER CLERK (CONT'D)
>   If you'd just like to see my
>   colleague...around the corner, that
>   would be great.

He points over. Howard and Jean obediently approach the
supervisor.

>   SUPERVISOR
>   (smiling pleasantly)
>   Hello. Would you come with me please...

                                      JEAN

What's wrong?

                                SUPERVISOR

Oh, absolutely nothing to worry about.

Jean is very worried. Howard puts a comforting hand on her shoulder. The supervisor leads them to a door marked "NO ENTRY". She punches in a code, and holds it open for them. Smiles at them as they pass.

INT. CORRIDOR.

They enter a long, bleak corridor. The three of them walk along in silence, coughing occasionally. Their footsteps echo. They go into a bare, tidy office.

INT. SUPERVISOR'S OFFICE.

The supervisor sits behind the desk, empty apart from a row of pens and marker pens. She motions to two chairs.

                                SUPERVISOR

Sit down.

She reads the file, carefully turning over the pages. Furrowing her brow, she selects a marker pen and ruler, draws a neat line through one of the pages.

                        SUPERVISOR (CONT'D)

About your application... there was just one little thing...

                              HOWARD

Well, I can't think what it would be... I -- I mean, we sometimes used to throw snails over the fence into the neighbour's garden but...
(remembering)
-- oh my God, Dirty CumSluts!

                                JEAN

What?

                    HOWARD
I once downloaded a porn site at work.

                    JEAN
How could you!

                    HOWARD
It was a joke -- Martin Wilks sent it
to me.

                    SUPERVISOR
I see. Two little things then.

She makes another careful note in the file.

                    SUPERVISOR (CONT'D)
No, the main problem's actually to do
with this impaling thousands of
innocent peasants on sharpened poles.

                    HOWARD
I'm sorry?

                    SUPERVISOR
Well, according to your file, you
impaled thousands of innocent peasants
on sharpened poles, condemning them to
a slow and lingering death. Now, my
guess is, this is probably going to
count against you --

                    HOWARD
Erm, I think you've got a bit mixed
up...

                    SUPERVISOR
Have we? Oh...

                    HOWARD
I didn't impale anyone on poles.

                    SUPERVISOR
Are you sure?

                         HOWARD
              Yes of course I'm sure!

                        SUPERVISOR
              What about when you worked at...
                        (consults file)
              Lambert Engineering...

                         HOWARD
              No!

                        SUPERVISOR
              Well you downloaded porn sites --

                         HOWARD
              Ye...yes...-- As a joke. ... look this
              is ridiculous, I have led an
              impeccable life.

                        SUPERVISOR
              I see. Well, I'm sure it's just a
              small administrational error...

                          JEAN
              So -- you'll sort it all out then...

                        SUPERVISOR
              What I suggest is that you go through
              to Mr Burrell.

                         HOWARD
              But --

              She hands back the file and directs them out.

                        SUPERVISOR
              Out of the door, turn left, second
              door on the right, okay?

              She gives them another of her brittle smiles.

INT. CORRIDOR -- MOMENTS LATER.

Howard and Jean come out of the office and walk uncertainly
down the corridor to the next door on the right. It's half
open. They peek in.

                    HOWARD
          Mr Burrell?

INT. MR BURRELL'S OFFICE.

Mr Burrell's desk is an unruly mess of paperwork, dirty
mugs and old paper plates. He's eating a bacon roll.

                    MR BURRELL
          Yes yes, come in, come in...

Mr Burrell is smiley and jolly, with damp patches under his
arms. He gets up and takes a pile of files off a chair.

                    MR BURRELL CONT'D)
          Yes, sit down. Just let me make some
          space.

He shifts some files off the chairs, chuckling happily to
himself.

                    MR. BURRELL
          Please...

He gestures for them to take a seat but just before they do
he notices the file Howard is carrying.

                    MR. BURRELL (CONT'D)
          So, that's for me is it?

He takes the file and sits back down taking another bite
out of the bacon roll.

                    MR. BURRELL (CONT'D)
          So, let's have a little look shall we.

He starts tapping letters into his computer with one hand
-- painfully slowly.

                    MR BURRELL CONT'D)
          Mr I-M-P-A-L-E-
                    (computer bleep)
          Oops... E- R. Mr Impaler!.

Jean looks at Howard. Howard clears his throat.

                    HOWARD
          Actually, it's not Mr Impaler in fact.
          In fact, it's Mr Whittam. Howard
          Whittam.

                         JEAN
          With a silent 'h'.

                    MR BURRELL

          So you're not...
          (reads off file) "Impaler...
          Vlad." Middle name "the",
          then?

                    HOWARD
          No. No, I'm a precision engineer. Vlad
          the Impaler was a vicious tyrant who
          impaled thousands of peasants on
          sharpened sticks.

                    MR BURRELL
          Well that's a coincidence -- that's
          exactly what you did.

                    HOWARD
          No, no I didn't, you see. Obviously
          there's been a mix up.

There's a pause. Mr Burrell takes a moment to absorb this
state of affairs.

                    MR BURRELL
          Whoops. I'm terribly sorry. It does
          happen occasionally -- pretty busy
          here today, as you can imagine!

He guffaws cheerily. Howard and Jean join in uneasily. He
takes another mouthful of the bacon roll.

> MR BURRELL (CONT'D)
> Oh dear!

> JEAN
> So you can change it then can you?

> MR BURRELL
> No, I can't. Best thing to do, quite
> honestly, is if you trot on down to
> Admin -- and they'll be able to sort
> it all out for you.

> JEAN
> But that lady said --

He ushers them out of a different door into another
endlessly long corridor.

> MR BURRELL
> Straight down the corridor and take
> the lift.

He takes a final bite of his roll and slams the door.

CUT TO:

INT. CORRIDOR TO LIFTS.

The Whittams walk down the corridor to the lifts. A MEMBER
OF STAFF comes by accompanied by someone that we glimpse as
HITLER.

> MEMBER OF STAFF
> (chatting)
> ... no, I haven't been to Moscow
> either, I hear it's amazing-ly
> cheap...wouldn't want to go in Winter
> though.

Howard and Jean enter the lift.

> JEAN
> Howard -- don't stand for it. You've
> got to sort this thing out.

> HOWARD
> I'm handling the situation Jean. Let's
> not get hysterical, it's not the end
> of the world --

He breaks off. PING! The lift arrives.

CUT TO:

INT. WAITING ROOM -- SHORT TIME LATER.

The lift doors open revealing Howard and Jean still
bickering.

> JEAN
> It's too late to send a letter --

> HOWARD
> I didn't say that!

Howard and Jean exit the lift and stop short. They're in an
oddly large and austere waiting room with lines of metal
chairs going off into the distance. On the table are old
magazines -- Punch and Women's Realm.
The Whittams obediently take a ticket from the dispenser
and sit down to wait their turn. Howard looks around. The
room is entirely empty, apart from the two of them.

A door opens. They look up hopefully and Howard gestures to
speak as A HARASSED CLERK strides past them with some
papers, then disappears through another door.

Presently a buzzer sounds and above the door a sign lights
up. NEXT CLIENT: VLAD THE IMPALER. The Whittams look round
but there's no-one else in the room.

> JEAN
> It's not you...

> HOWARD
> Of course it's not.

Pause. The sign flashes again, a bit louder and brighter.
Agitated, Howard gets up.

> HOWARD (CONT'D)
> Oh this is ridiculous. Come on...

He straightens his shirt and is about to just walk in
assertively, but decides against it and taps gently on the
door. They hear a muffled "come in."

INT. SUPERVISOR'S OFFICE.

Howard and Jean walk in and stop short. They realise they
are back in the supervisor's office. The supervisor is on a
chair, reaching up with a window pole, trying to open a
window.

Howard and Jean look at each other. The supervisor turns,
fanning herself as she steps down.

> SUPERVISOR
> Isn't it hot in here!

She parks the pole against the wall, goes back to her desk.

> HOWARD
> Er, look, we've been told -- and I'm
> actually -- I'm getting a little bit
> cross now-

> JEAN
> This really should've been sorted out -

> HOWARD
> Jean, Jean, I'm handling this.

> SUPERVISOR
> Please, try to stay calm, Mr. Impaler.

> HOWARD
> For the last time, I am not Vlad the
> Impaler! I am Howard Whittam!

                         JEAN
         With a silent 'h'!

                        HOWARD
         I am Howard Whittam with a silent "h",
         and I have had a very ordinary, very
         well-behaved, in fact, very dull life.
         Oh yes, dull!

He gets up agitatedly.

                    HOWARD (CONT'D)
         Have you any idea what it was like,
         not doing anything bad -- for which
         read, anything enjoyable -- for year
         after year? Do you realise on New
         Year's Eve in 1993 Martin Wilks' wife
         offered me a blow job? (Jean gasps)
         But I declined. Oh yes. Some stupid,
         mistaken sense of propriety made me
         hold back -- and it wasn't just that
         New Year's eve either --- my whole
         life! I never took drugs. I never
         overtook on the inside lane. I never
         ran naked through a graveyard. Because
         I perhaps foolishly believed in a
         sense of divine Justice, of being
         rewarded for a life well lived. In
         other words, because I knew this day
         would come -- I didn't, on New Year's
         Eve...

He's more desperate than angry.

                    HOWARD (CONT'D)
         So please, sort this out. You can't
         send me to Hell, you just can't!

The supervisor looks at Howard, a little puzzled.

                      SUPERVISOR
         I'm sorry, there's obviously been a
         terrible misunderstanding...

                    HOWARD
          Yes...

                    SUPERVISOR
          You see, you already are in Hell. Both
          of you.

Pause. The Whittams are stunned.

                    JEAN
          But... that's not fair!

                    SUPERVISOR
          Well that's the thing about Hell, Mrs
          Impaler -- it's not fair.

Howard sinks back into his chair, realisation dawning.
After a moment's pause, the supervisor gently pushes the
file back across the desk.

                    SUPERVISOR (CONT'D)
          Now, what I suggest you do is take
          this file through to Mr Burrell...

                    HOWARD
          Mr Burrell?

                    SUPERVISOR
          Yes, sort it out with Mr Burrell.

She gives one of her brittle smiles.

INT. CORRIDOR.

POV down the corridor. The camera lingers on the FIRE EXIT.

                    HEAVEN STAFF MEMBER (O.S.)
          Welcome to Heaven, Mr Whittam...

INT. STAFF MEMBER'S OFFICE.

A pleasant, white-themed office. The pleasant, white-themed
staff member holds out a hand to VLAD THE IMPALER, still
dressed in full armour.

                    HEAVEN STAFF MEMBER
          We've decided -- under the
          circumstances -- to overlook the
          Filthy Cumsluts incident...

The smiling clerk impales a pink form on a desk spike...

                    THE END

Poems

Roy Woolley

Minotaur

The found him in the guts of the city
on one of our holy nights. Zoned-out.
Lost to the world. Face to the wall.
Done over by locals looking for sport.

Still yelling when the cops arrived.
Two guys on the graveyard shift
who clocked him once and called for backup.
Later, darts from a zookeeper's gun

shut him down, locked him into a dream
only I could wake him from.
Records say that three men were needed
to load him onto the gurney

but I remember a delicacy of step,
a calm appraisement of the contours
of my face, his aching awareness
of what was still to come.

Reading Marx

The walls are so packed with angels
I'll need to call a builder. For the moment though,
that call can wait. I'm speeding in a taxi
towards the city centre, towards an assignation

I can't afford to miss. Not with colleagues or spies
but with an old love, one I though long gone.
Days in the labyrinth, nights in the forest -
these were the things we shared for a while

in the dog-days of summer. Riot-time,
strikes in the city, an army on stand-by.
I wanted to fight for freedom and he did too.
We studied Marx together at night school.

He fell for the instructor and, after days
of tearful espionage, I realized I'd lost him.
I returned to our cast-off plans, our thoughts
of a new life high in the trees, away from it all.

The taxi is going faster than I thought possible.
Offices, a massage-parlour above a sex-shop,
an emporium of dog-fighting paraphernalia
speed by so quickly their colours blur

and I cover my eyes with a newspaper.
The text of the world this close is a revelation.
Even the space between words hums with meaning
like this rugby-team of angels breathing down my neck.

Loki in TV

In his first role he was simply one among many.
The victim of an explosion at an oil-refinery.
The scenery smoked as he lay breathing,
hardly moving as the camera panned.

He lay with the dead in three later episodes.
In the first his skull was shaved the better to show
the deep abrasions caused by masonry.
In the second he was stabbed, in the third set alight.

These roles continued for several years and, each time,
he felt himself nearing the end, the act
over-taking the actor. Adept at feigning stillness
he was soon practising the death agonies of strangers,

the screams of the violently injured.
He studied in mirrors the wounds they made him wear;
the deep gash in his neck from a gangland vendetta,
the bullet-hole blown into his forehead

by a teenager strung out on amphetamines.
Soon they'll want him discovered
in some suburban basement for a copper to find,
an elderly pathologist to mis-identify.

Continuity

The wolves won't run together or, if they run,
don't arrive at the camp simultaneously.

If this doesn't happen, the camp-fire won't be lit
and without this heat, surrounding trees won't be scorched.

If they're not scorched, then there's no black
to scrape off, no way to signal a path to the village

and the village, under siege, will only last a few more days
before a rocket fired eight miles offshore

reduces to bone and ash eight families, forty lives.
Then the actors will not turn away and the music for the scene

will be impossible to write. The musicians, at a loose end,
pass the time drinking and gambling in Stuttgart.

And so the back-story won't be filmed, like the time
your man in the studio was drawn back through silence

to a childhood stage-managed by dreams.
Wolf prints through the house. Streaming red tongues.

Glitterbug

i.m.

We pointed our cameras at the future and waited.
Not even Prospero dreaming in his cell
could have imagined the colours of the city
I caught that morning high above the Thames.

Everything flowed in those days or was beginning to.
We experimented with radical drag, watched six-hour
silent films of someone's lover sleeping,
became alternative Miss Worlds

as our shame retreated into the dark
and left us the light to parade in.
Petrol-bombs and direct action, banners and protests.
A government obsessed with a past

we refused to recognise. Signs of the times.
Vietnam unravelled behind newsprint on the floor
as friends devised mechanical ballets
that took years to compose and an hour to perform.

We fashioned masks with materials we'd stolen
and entombed dollar-bills in plastic capes
we wore to all-night discos. In my first feature
friends recited Latin under the Sicilian sun.

Later, I imagined my country burning and broken,
ruled by a naked king in Rotherhithe.
Random violence and the love of violence.
Impossible loves retreating with a neutron's speed.

I watched my own death on TV, a tombstone
endlessly falling. Cat-calls. Attacks in the press.
An actress sinking her teeth into an actor's neck.
The rage I worked into my final pictures.

The Pale Stenographer

I am charged with several offences
such as disturbing the water's uncomplicated flow
and attaching too much importance
to the swaying reeds and the complacent mud.

The clerk hovers beneath a wave
and reaches into its swaying crest
to retrieve a notebook or glasses to peer
at the court usher miles below.

A bracelet of samphire eats into my ankle
as the spherical clusters of my words
are recorded by the pale stenographer
whose small head is nodding slightly.

The rain too, offers its testimony,
gliding into the courtroom to take the stand.
It has seen everything and forgets nothing.
Not my silence or my late night rants

about the treatment of snow
or the undue weight given to the iceberg's decay.
I spoke with the passion of a tropical downpour
until I was caught by the waves and consumed.

Whale Memory

The man with the harpoon
painted on blue background

is the guardian of these canvas chairs,
this wooden stage

lit by an oil-lamp.
Perhaps someone sells programmes.

But what's next in the sequence
is wordless and in the semi-shade

cast by an oil-lamp.
The dark blaze of the whale's skin,

the yellow and white of the wound
unhealed in his right side.

The coils and coils of rope are a foot away
from my own and my father's hands.

3am Garden

Hi Tom. Sorry for bailing out
last Friday. There was something
I'd been planning for ages. Remember Sarah?
Well, it was nothing to do with her

but the dragon she was keeping
in an apple-crate with a brick on top.
Sod her I thought. She's no right
to treat anything like that.

Did you catch my talk on freedom
and responsibility last week?
'Don't mention the police. I *am* the police'.
So me, the dragon and the night

in my ex's 3am garden.
No light from her window,
only the glow from my mobile to help.
Well, the creature was fast asleep

and the straw it slept on singed and dirty.
For some reason she'd placed a picture
of St George on the lid. I wrapped the brick in it
before lobbing the lot over the fence

into the neighbour's patch. A philosophy student
writing on Heidegger and the revolution
that never was, at least in my time.
The dragon's scales were small,

curled around his spine like a sheath,
red veins pulsing through the green.
Rain was falling as I wrapped it in my coat.
It was warm as toast.

Poems

Greg Delanty

from *The Greek Anthology, Book XVII*

Lulu's Family Diner

I'm lucky enough to get a window seat

    overlooking the mountains, north of Adamsville Plain.

The country is a platinum blonde, dyed by Fall.

    Lulu hums a country song, serves me home fries

the shade of the countryside. She tells me to make myself at home.

    Lulu is the beautiful muse of what they call homely.

I think I have a crush on her. She returns, asks

    if I want a refill. I tell her the home fries were the best

ever. This makes Lulu, lonely Lulu, lovely Lulu, happy.

    Not many can say they made a muse feel good?

Not many had a muse call them "Honey"?

John the Maker

from *The Greek Anthology, Book XVII*
Weather Relief

After days of unusual fine weather, a cloud
    settles like a hood on the peninsula, shuts out
this renowned ragged coastline:
    mythical islands, beaches, windy roads, tropical flora.
We're relieved of the sense something in us can't
    match such unsettling splendor, bringing home to us
we're more at home in this cloud-shrouded shore,
    that life now is more clearly bearable.

Gregory of Corkus

The Essence of Sandalwood

Stephanie Chong

Extract from a novel, *The Essence of Sandalwood*.
Inspired by the life of Matya Kotlier (1956-2006).

The Essence of Sandalwood

Prologue

Milena

I sit and wait, the only white woman crowded in amongst the Tibetans. This is the latest stop on my tour of temples, spiritual healers, shamans, and snake-oil peddlers. In this shabby basement apartment, the smoky-sweet scent of sandalwood lingers. I wonder how many sticks of incense have been burned here, how many prayers have been offered to this statue of Buddha. His flaking gold paint makes him look like a refugee from an enlightened realm, taking a beating here on earth.

I have come here to be blessed by a Rinpoche who's making the rounds of the Tibetan communities in North America to raise money for his monastery. He's spent the last two years in a cave, the Tibetans say. They say that during those years, he got his energy not from food, but from eating rocks.

'Sonam's cancer disappeared after the Rinpoche blessed him,' one of the Tibetans says. The others nod. There are more stories of illnesses healed, of miraculous powers the Rinpoche possesses.

A door opens, and a young man comes out, a translator. He points at me. 'The Rinpoche will see you now.'

Someone squeezes my hand. 'Good luck.'

I smile back. It isn't luck I need; it's a miracle.

The Rinpoche is an enormously fat man, sitting on a bare mattress on the floor, a couple of blankets piled on top of him. He is wrapped in robes of deep beet-red punctuated by a swath of orange. I offer him the white scarf I've brought. He chants a blessing over me, a stream of impossibly low vowel tones that vibrates through my body, calming, soothing. He places the scarf around my neck.

'Do you have any questions for the Rinpoche?' the translator asks.

The question pops out of my mouth, almost of its own accord: 'What is the purpose of my life?'

It's the question that has been haunting me lately, now that I've left my career. Mother, wife. Those are roles that are rewarding, but I've always thought there must be more to life, some deeper meaning or goal that explains it all. What that meaning or goal is, I can't even begin to imagine.

A benevolent smile passes over the Rinpoche's face. He speaks rapidly in Tibetan, and the translator interprets. 'He says he is very happy that you have come here so young to follow the path of the dharma. The purpose of your life is to tear away the veil of illusion to understand the true nature of reality.'

It's a good answer, a stock Buddhist response, but not the answer I wanted to hear. I hide my disappointment behind a smile.

'Do you have any healings you would like the Rinpoche to perform?' the translator asks.

'I have stage four breast cancer. It's spread to my spine,' I say.

The Rinpoche nods. The translator explains, 'There are two methods of healing. The gentle method, and the wrathful method. On you, he will use the gentle method. Please take off your shirt.'

I remember the black lace bra I'm wearing under my shirt. My cheeks burn. I know I'm lucky I still have to worry about exposing my breasts. Or maybe unlucky. A mastectomy was not an option because the cancer had already spread too far by the time I was diagnosed. 'Um, I…'

Both of them look back at me with expressions of perfect calm.

The translator blinks. 'Don't worry. The Rinpoche is enlightened. He has no sexual feelings whatsoever. If you like, I can leave the room,' he says.

I nod. The translator leaves, and I unbutton my shirt.

Lying across the bed in front of the Rinpoche, I feel ridiculous and vaguely pornographic: a woman in a black lace bra, lying on a bed, exposed before a stranger's eyes.

But the Rinpoche demonstrates no interest in my half-naked body as he picks up a bronze, spoon-shaped metal object from a small table. I watch as he blows on it a few times, heating it with his breath. When he touches it to my spine, it is burning hot. I want to scream. The pain is intense, and I wonder briefly whether I'm going to faint.

Finally, it is over. I get up, pull on my shirt. The Rinpoche puts the spoon instrument back on the table and smiles his munificent smile.

When the translator comes back, he tells me, 'The Rinpoche says that the cancer is not healed, but that he has stopped its progression. The disease will not advance before he returns in six months.'

At home, I show Diego the burn marks. He says, 'If that's the gentle method, what the hell is the wrathful method?'

As we lie together in bed that night, he cradles my body. It's the weight of my head on his chest that I want him to remember. The feel of my hair, thinned from the chemo treatments, but still curling and soft. In the dark, I reach up to trace the line of his jaw, re-learning the rasp of the stubble of his beard beneath my fingertips.

Wrapped in my husband's arms, my mind churns over the Rinpoche's words. To discover the true nature of reality is undoubtedly a worthy goal. But I still need to figure out who I am. What it is I'm doing here.

Inside me, a voice whispers, '*Fight.*'

Chapter One

Milena, six months earlier

Welcome to the War Room.

We warhorses wear designer suits; our stable has plate glass windows that look out from an office tower's forty-fifth floor onto a stunning view of Toronto's waterfront. On a clear day, sailboats dot the waters of the harbour. The CN tower, that beacon of an architectural monstrosity, looms to the right of us. But we can't see a thing right now, because fog clouds the windows. It's getting dark and we might as well be sealed in an iron box. An oblong table of polished mahogany is spread with the plans and strategies for waging combat. Or rather, for launching a lawsuit.

Despite its name, this room has nothing to do with *real* war. It's just a boardroom in a law firm where we keep documents related to trials. The files piled on the table are only made of paper. There's nothing in sight that might explode, no exposed flesh wounds, no coppery reek of blood. In our world, death and dismemberment are only metaphors and images, not reality. Here, a single lost life might be grounds for a six-year court battle. We think we're tough, but up here in the rarefied air of Greenfield Patterson, we're insulated from real violence. We'd scream or go crazy if we ever caught a whiff of real death.

My face is greasy with the sheen of staying up too late every night this week. The air in my lungs has long gone stale. My back aches from sitting in this chair for far too many hours in a row. But I'm still functioning. Still billing, still bartering my life away in six-minute increments.

The door bursts open, and Ernie Weinstein struts in. Ernie is a twenty-year-old man trapped inside the pot-bellied body of a forty-three-year-old. His brown hair is slightly rumpled, and his tie is thrown over his shoulder in a gesture of rebellion against authority. Ernie hasn't realised yet that he *is* authority – a partner in this prestigious law firm. Here in this boardroom, there are three other lawyers. We are all grown adults and fully qualified professionals. But every one of us is beholden to Ernie's whims. We're lucky that he's a benevolent dictator. We play along with his pretences because it's less embarrassing for everyone that way.

He crashes into the chair next to me and puts his feet up on the unblemished wood of the table. Instead of saying hello, the first thing out of his mouth is a moan. 'Ross, I'm getting old,' he says. Ernie never uses my first name because it reminds him that I'm a woman.

In the pause that follows, I realise that he's waiting for the magic words. Without them, the conversation will not progress. 'You're not getting old, Ernie,' I say. Sometimes working with this man is like babysitting.

He peers over at the expert's report I'm analysing. 'How's it coming with Dr Silver?'

The expert report confirms yet again that our client, Dr Kenneth Silver, is as guilty as the Butcher of Fleet Street. During half a dozen routine surgeries, Dr Silver's drinking problem got the better of his medical training. One patient went in for a tonsillectomy and ended up in a coma for seven months. Another had laser surgery to correct snoring, but ended up with an infection so serious it caused irreversible brain damage. Dr Silver exhibits no guilt about any of this. He is seventy years old, now mercifully retired, and in complete denial. Somehow, in the process of litigation, Dr Silver's guilt has become my problem, instead of his. My problem, Ernie's problem, and the problem of the three other lawyers here, all of us poring over medical records in an effort to untangle the snarl of Dr Silver's medical negligence.

So, when Ernie asks how it's going, the answer is as follows: *I want to scream and burn the War Room to the ground, along with every document related to these godforsaken cases. That's how it's going.* But

163

I don't dare voice this to Ernie.

Instead, I smile and say, 'Fine, Ernie.'

'Great. Another claim came in today,' he says. He tosses another thick court document on the table. We gather like buzzards over a dead body. I pick up the claim and flip through it as Ernie narrates: 'It's a botched tracheotomy. Silver went in to remove a cyst from the plaintiff's windpipe, and ended up nicking her vocal cords. She's claiming she can't speak, suing for five million dollars. Let's request the medical reports, find an expert witness to give us an opinion. You know the drill.'

There's a collective groan. The most junior of us, Clayton, is an earnest young man who looks like a kid dressed up in his father's suit. He says, 'Just what we need – another victim of the butcher.'

Another trial coming down the line. I think about the approaching summer, when Diego and I are planning on taking Gabriela, our five-year-old daughter, to Disneyland for the first time. Our summer holiday begins to crumble before my eyes.

Ernie heaves himself up from his chair. 'We'll get there. Keep up the good work, team,' he says in an apathetic tone. He may be a genius at the law, but a people manager he's not.

As I settle back into my expert report, Ernie turns, poised to yank open the boardroom door. 'Especially you, Ross. Keep it up, and it'll be a smooth ride on the partnership track this year.' He winks, then swings out the door.

Oh, the partnership track. Seven years ago, when I joined this firm, I vowed I would leave before it came to this. *Someone shoot me if I ever make partner*, I used to say. The idea of sacrificing my life, my time with my family, made me shudder. I have no idea what happened, but seven years have passed in the haze of exhaustion that has become my permanent state of being. Ernie's comment is no big surprise – the partners have been whispering about cutting me a slice of the pie for the last two years.

Now, I have no idea whether to be excited or depressed. I guess I'm a little of both. I hate this job, but I love it, too. The complexity of the work fascinates me, and so does the thrill of the high-stakes cases. But sometimes I wish the work were a little *less* complex and *less* thrilling.

I wish had a little more time to breathe.

The boardroom phone rings, and Clayton picks it up. 'Milena, it's your kid.'

I greet my daughter in hushed tones. I might as well be speaking a foreign language in this room full of aggression and jargon.

'Mommy! Where are you?' It's less a question than an accusation. Gabriela is a smart kid. She dialled this number; she knows I'm at work.

I say patiently, 'Mommy's working, sweetheart.'

'You were supposed to pick me up for my ballet lesson,' she wails.

Shit. Each of the last three Wednesdays, I've hauled my tired ass out of bed at five-thirty in the morning so I could leave work early to shuttle the kidlet to dance class. This morning, I left the house early, as planned. I have already billed eight hours today; I was planning on billing another hour or two at home tonight. I had intended to leave at four o'clock. I glance at my watch: it's already four-fifteen. Something must have slipped. I'm so fatigued this week that the synapses just aren't firing like they should.

'Can Dar take you?' I say. Darlene, our housekeeper, is sometimes more of a mother to my daughter than I am. It's a reality that I try my best to ignore.

There's a little sniffle on the other end of the line. I imagine Gabriela standing in the front hallway of our house, outfitted in her dance clothes, her skinny little leotarded body bundled under her winter coat. 'Dar's cooking dinner. You're supposed to pick me up.'

In my mind's eye, I see her lower lip tremble. She's getting ready to cry. It's not her fault that I'm a terrible mother. 'Put her on the phone, honey.'

There is no trace of recrimination in the housekeeper's voice, even though there should be. She doesn't judge me. Or else she's an excellent actress. Either way, I count myself lucky to have her. She agrees to take Gabriela to her ballet lesson in a taxi – I will meet them there and drive them home.

I bolt down the hallway to my office, grab my coat, dodging my assistant and the hundred-and-one phone messages that have piled up while I've been in the War Room.

On my way out, I run into Ernie in the hallway. 'Where are you off to?' he says.

'Ballet lessons,' I say.

He gives me a sceptical once-over. 'Hate to break it to you, but it's a bit late for a career change.'

'I have to pick up my daughter.' I get into the elevator, pushing the button and imagining it has the power to switch Ernie off.

Ernie nods, trying to be sympathetic, but as the elevator doors slide shut, I see the disapproval on his face. He has children of his own, but it's his wife who runs his home life. He has never taken six months off to care for an infant. He has never left work early to pick up a child.

What I need is a wife running *my* home life. Diego is the love of my life, but is unlikely to turn househusband anytime soon.

I sink against the elevator's slick panelling and stare at the weather report on the flatscreen TV monitor. Snow is forecast every day this week.

As the elevator descends forty-five stories, it seems as though the partnership track is heading onward and upward without me. But I know I've made the right choice. At least today, I have.

By some miracle, there's a parking spot on the busy street in front of the ballet school. As I walk into the building, I force myself to breathe a little deeper. I haven't left the city, but it's a different world in here. The high, vaulted ceilings and the slightly musty smell of old building are a universe away from the War Room.

The wooden staircase creaks beneath my high-heeled boots as I walk up to the viewing gallery. A handful of girls in their early teens thump down the stairs, their hair tightly scraped back in buns, all rangy adolescence and giggles. They're straight out of a Degas painting, but with bubblegum and cell phones.

On the second-floor balcony, I find Darlene looking down at the row of five-year-olds trying to lift their little pointed feet in unison. I put my hand on her shoulder in a wordless gesture of thanks.

I watch the kids freestyle around the studio, mimicking the movements of grown-up dancers. They twirl endlessly in front of the big mirrors, sometimes falling in graceless heaps like tired-out puppies flopping on the ground after too much play.

There is a shuffle of ballet-slippered feet padding up the staircase. Gabriela comes hurtling toward me, throws her arms around me. 'Mommy, did you see me?' She is full of chatter about the class, the teacher, how she wants to be a ballerina when she grows up. She tilts her face up toward me, her elfin features lit with pleasure. Her face is a miniature version of mine, but my features are delicately rendered in her child-perfect skin. Instead of my blue eyes, she looks back at me with Diego's limpid brown ones. And she doesn't have my tangly auburn hair, but her father's dark, straight tresses.

I lean down and gather her to me. The sugary scent of baby shampoo rises from her hair. We still use it because she's not ready for the real stuff. In so many ways, she's still a baby. I secretly wish there were some way to tuck her back inside my body and keep her there, safe and protected.

At home, we gather around the Chinese takeout that Diego has picked up to replace the unbaked lasagne Dar has relegated to the fridge until tomorrow. Gabriela insists on using chopsticks, stabbing ferociously at her food until I intervene with a fork.

We're tired, all three of us, Gabriela sagging noticeably in her chair once the chopsticks have been taken away. *Is this what it's like to have it all?* I wonder. A job I love (to hate), a gorgeous (albeit exhausted) husband, a beautiful (but slightly sullen) daughter. The only thing I don't have is time. But we're all here, together, and that's what's important.

Across our dining-room table, Diego reaches for the Ma Po chicken. 'What did you do with my tie, Gabriela?' he asks, knowing that it's lying somewhere in the family room amongst her toys; she ran off with it while we were setting the table. Her little face lights up, then she collapses into giggles, almost falling off her chair.

While the two of them banter and joke across the table, my thoughts drift back to work. Mentally, I am in my office, sorting through Dr Silver's case, wondering how we're going to manage another claim. I worry whether we're going to have enough manpower to deal with everything in the coming months. Maybe we should pull another associate onto the team...

Diego's voice snaps me back to the present. 'How was your day, sweetheart?'

'Fine,' I say, embarrassed to be caught worrying about work at the dinner table.

He smiles at me with those cinnamon-roast eyes of his, so full-bodied they are almost aromatic. Diego is beautiful, but he'll never realise how beautiful. He's too much of a pragmatist to dwell on himself. I guess he's had to be. A decade in Canada has softened, but not erased the effects of his childhood in Colombia.

We met at a refugee law clinic, when he'd first arrived in this country. When I was an idealistic young law student volunteering for a summer, keen on saving the world. Diego always says that I rescued him, pulled him out the refuse like a tarnished old pocket watch on a flea market junk table. Brought him home and polished him up.

But Diego needed no polishing. Even back then, he shone. He may have been poor, but he was magnificent nonetheless. Ten years on, his skin, once tawny and burnished by the scorch of the Colombian sun, has faded to a more sedate tone beneath the fluorescent lights of his office. These days, he maintains his physique from gym workouts. His father's farm, where he spent his youth working the land, is now the battleground of guerrilla forces and drug lords.

Here in Canada, this country built by immigrants, Diego may have become genericised, melded into the grand mosaic of cultures we pride ourselves on. But he is safe, and I would even dare to say he's successful. He's devoted to his job as a business analyst. It has left dark circles beneath his eyes, but he never complains about it. Unlike me, Diego tries to hide his exhaustion.

He's a survivor, this husband of mine.

I watch them at the dinner table, their two dark heads bent to study the little white slips of paper cracked from the shells of the fortune cookies.

Diego sounds out the words on Gabriela's fortune. 'Your greatest wish will soon be fulfilled,' he says, drawing out each of the syllables as he points.

'Maybe that means I'll have a baby sister this year,' our daughter crows.

Over the table, I meet Diego's wide, surprised gaze, and feel my lips curve into a smile. This is no new request. Last Christmas, when she woke up and rushed to the tree, she was visibly disappointed with the array of gifts laid out there. It took me ten minutes to pry the reason out of her: she'd asked Santa for a new baby, and he hadn't brought one. Thankfully, she was distracted by unwrapping her toys, shreds of green, red and gold wrapping paper flying everywhere. And she quickly forgot about the baby.

But now, it strikes me that I *would* like to have another child. The thought has been ruminating in my head for a while – for years, if I'm honest with myself. Work has kept us both so busy that we rarely talk about it, except as a vague possibility at an indeterminate future date. But Gabriela is five years old already, and getting set in the ways of an only child.

Still, if I make partner this year, maybe that will be the time to do it. Ernie's promise looms in my mind. Partnership would mean another level of job security. The possibility of another child dangles before my eyes, a baby-shaped carrot with pink-and-blue knitted booties on its carrot feet.

Lying in bed later that night, I say to Diego, 'Let's have another one.'

He stops typing, hands poised above the laptop he frequently takes to bed with us. 'Another what? Chinese take-out? That was good.'

'Don't be silly. You know what I'm talking about. Another *baby*,' I say. 'We're not getting any younger, you know.' As the words come out of my mouth, I realise I've been spending too much time around Ernie. *I'm getting old.*

He sets the laptop aside, switches off the lamp on the nightstand. 'Milena, you're thirty-three. We had Gabriela so young. Let's wait another couple of years. Or a year, at least. Until you make partner,' he coaxes as he pulls the covers over us.

I know he's right. When we got married, we were practically children ourselves – by today's standards, anyway.

Yes, he's right. Now is not the ideal time to have another baby. If we had one now, I would be self-sabotaging my shot at partnership, making my life unnecessarily difficult by adding another set of responsibilities into the mix. 'A year isn't so long to wait. I want her to have someone to play with,' I say.

'Gabriela will be fine. She has all her little friends at school. She's a perfectly well adjusted kid.'

I continue, undeterred. 'Maybe I should start taking folic acid. You're supposed to start taking it a year before you get pregnant, anyway.'

'Stop worrying so much about everything,' Diego sighs, nestling into me. 'Get some rest.'

'I'm going to make a doctor's appointment. I'm due for a physical soon, anyway.'

'Mmm.' It's not a *yes*, but it's not a *no* either. He's already drifting into slumber, and I don't dare push the issue any further.

But I'm so excited, I can barely sleep.

Fidelity

Tim Pears

Fidelity

The white sheets, and the pillowcases, are freshly laundered. Hung to dry on the line out in the garden, they have brought the optimism of the open air to the bed. He is naked.

Sarah wanders between rooms. Remembering things, chores to be done. Toys are picked up from a floor; small clothes chosen, laid out for the morning. She removes her trousers, hangs them on the towel rail beside the chest of drawers, then remembers something else; roams from one room to another in states of undress. Her still black hair. He watches his wife from the bed: the tasks, combined with her memory, its lapses and recalls, create an erotic display for him.

In the bathroom her body. Nails clipped, cream applied, hairs pulled; she is in there tending herself, with the calm of a gardener. The toilet flushes. Taps run.

Here on her table: half-filled crosswords and su dokus; a digital alarm clock; the mug of water he brought upstairs. Outside, the whoosh of traffic noise on Woodstock Road: the sound of waves approaching, breaking on sand, receding. The sky is a darkening blue. Naked, he waits for her.

The girl he did not notice at first. Beauty was not enough in itself to distract him. Nor was youth. He wasn't sure. It was only when her intelligence became apparent that he fell.

There were certain points to ram home. Show Don't Tell. Detail. What moves you, really? Use all your senses. Again: Detail.

Then at the same moment, in the fifth or sixth week, almost every member of the class produced similarly, competent, touching stories. Often they involved grandparents. The difference between the talented one or two and the rest, evident from day one, became blurred. Only the really obtuse or confused student fell back, marooned, unaware of being so: one short story set during the English Civil War, the death of a Roundhead volunteer. His life passed in front of his eyes like a film.

Strange, though, how he could grade her, her work, with dispassion. If there was any shift of perspective he could not detect it. He was proud of himself for this.

A new term, a new year, will start soon.

Sarah arrives in time at this space, two, three metres square, their home within their home. He pulls her to him and he tells her with his voice and with his body that he needs her, wants her, must have her. He makes his bodily strength apparent, his assertion the reassurance she requires that she is wanted.

She is tired. He kisses her. Strokes skin; caresses flesh. Feels in her kiss the decision taken, to proceed.

She was gifted, the student, that was certain. He thought of the dross he'd produced at her age, and shuddered. Perhaps her ability stirred a vampiric element to his desire: he imagined vanquishing her, taking unto himself her power as right of conquest.

Her rapture a surrender, of her talent to him.

The opposite was also true: she would squeeze him dry, suck the last dregs of his talent from him, render him obsolete. Succeed him.

Talent was important, it was the only thing that mattered. Rare and precious. Actually, it was two a penny, weren't there any number of talented writers, most of whom failed to flourish? Talent was worthless without persistence. If she lacked either will or stamina to carry on through inevitable rejection, and periods of dullness, and despair, then her talent would come to be seen as misleading: something others wrongfully encouraged, or an unfair self-deception.

*

Sarah's September tan. The pale soft areas of her body neglected, uninvited, but private, theirs alone now.

She will shower in the morning. The smell now and the taste of her. She brings her lived-in body to him. The remnants of her day, its exertions, are in the crevices, the folds, of her skin.

The student had wide shoulders. Pert nose, hooded eyes, suspicious, shy, arrogant. Self-absorbed in a way that talent, intelligence, youth assumed forgiveness of. She rarely smiled, even or especially at other people's wit. Gave little of herself away. Gave little. She was hieratic, aloof, inscrutable. So young; age might do anything , preserve her as she was, now, or turn her into someone else. Because of his attention, his desire, aching towards her, he could not help but see her gestures, her attention, as directed towards him. A provocative languidity.

He wants to make it new. He tries with inarticulate tongue, with clumsy, inadequate hands, to fashion a sentence addressed to his wife alone, a sentence that will make her senses bloom. It is beyond him. He both cleaves to and abandons her. She is on her own. When at last Sarah tenses, groaning, pushing him away, she is transformed. Muscles asserting themselves, rippling up through soft flesh to the surface.

Her wide shoulders he came to see as exemplary. Wide shouldered women had style, didn't they? Class. Swagger, almost. She could have stepped out of a photograph of the Cote d'Azur in nineteen-twenty-five, bronzed, newly married, smoking on the esplanade. Young and hard. The world was hers for the taking.

He rises up her body, they kiss. Her face is flushed. He delivers the taste of her from his mouth to hers, his lips to her tongue, as if she desired to know the taste but needed him to circumvent her ambivalence.

His desire quickens.

They become one now. Again. The familiarity of their fit. The bedstead complains. Sarah's eyes are closed, she could be anywhere, he doesn't know. He bends towards her neck, grasps her head, hides.

The girl was naked, but still she was proud. She knew, somehow, that she possessed riches which had been his, but were leaching from him. Time was dragging him, spiralling his energies away from her. He knelt, clutched her legs, pulled her down, and she fell, laughing, laughing at him.

Sarah opens her eyes, they are narrowed, does she see him?

He is hers. The world is irresistible. Barriers crumble.

He is gasping.

He rolls off her. They lie asunder. His lungs crave equilibrium; silence. He hears their son, in his room across the landing, yawn in his sleep.

What did he hope for from his students? That they would become more involved readers, of course. That they would enjoy writing as they might enjoy playing the piano. They all expected publication, though; money, fame. She too, yes of course, why not?

Clothes pulled back on. Outside, he rolls a cigarette. The nights are not yet cold. The sun has set behind Wytham Woods and their garden is bathed in a yellow light. He has poured into this glass what was left in the bottle, the last of the wine brought back from Cahors. The long night drive to the ferry.

On the crossing over, on the way to their holiday, he had taken their daughter out on deck: sea-bright sun, foam and spray and salt air, dazzle and power, the huge boat throbbing through deep water. What would her imagination make of this, he wondered. Would it provide her with material for the rest of her life? She spent the first days in the Dordogne saying, 'When are we going on the ship, Daddy? I want to go on the ship.'

The light in the garden fades, from yellow to gray. There is sound. No, not sound, movement. Is there? Perhaps not. He smokes, an occasional cigarette. She smoked on the Cote d'Azur. No, on the bench outside the college chapel, the student, alone, aloof from her fellows he glimpsed her back in June. Talent and loneliness. She sent out an invitation, spun from her pen into the air, offering him nothing, inviting him only to see her and be glad and make of her what he might.

He realises suddenly that the movement is on the lawn, a few feet away from him. A small animal, it's a hedgehog. What is it doing? Strange motion. Perhaps it is sweeping the grass, looking for insects. What a shame his son and daughter are asleep. His mother once woke his sisters and himself and took them to watch badgers, in a sett in the woods behind their home. Recollected wonder. Yes! He will go and wake the boy now. He stands. The hedgehog scuttles off into the gloom.

Should you write what you know? they asked.

What's important is what you know while you're writing. He told them the story of Maxim Gorky, whose scream brought his wife rushing to his study. She found him on the floor, clutching his stomach. He'd been writing a story in which a man stabs his wife.

Love all your characters, he said. He saw their scepticism. Identify with them, every one.

He admitted once telling Louis de Bernières how he must have enjoyed the research into hallucinogenic drugs for his South American trilogy. De Bernières looked at him with pity, perhaps contempt, and said that we were blessed with imagination, were we not?

'I'll bet he did,' the girl said, unsmiling. 'Never believe a writer.'

Be true to yourself, he said to them, opening his hands. Your way of seeing.

'Be true.' How easy it was to say.

He spits out toothpaste. It is red with blood. No, not blood, wine. He stares at himself. He thinks he has come up now, onto some plateau of contentment. A place that is and will continue to be ridiculous. He will reach the far side of this plateau if he is lucky, that is all. There will be no more progress, only children, growing.

He lowers the seat and the lid of the toilet before flushing it in the silent house. Closes the bathroom door.

His daughter is sleeping. She looks exhausted, as if sleep itself is tiring her. Floating, dreams swell in her vacant head, the ocean in all its surging immensity surrounds her.

His wife too seems to be asleep now. She has left his light on. He slides into bed. As he settles his body on the firm mattress she murmurs. He stretches out an arm, and switches off the light.

'Banyan'

Sudeep Sen

Banyan

As winter secrets
  melt

with the purple
  sun,

what is revealed
  is electric —

notes tune
  unknown scales,

syntax alters
  tongues,

terracotta melts
  white,

banyan ribbons
  into armatures

as branch-roots
  twist, meeting

soil in a circle.
  Circuits

glazed
  under cloth

carry
  alphabets

for a calligrapher's
 nib

italicised
 in invisible ink,

letters never
 posted,

cartographer's
 map, uncharted —

as phrases fold
 so do veils.

'Leave-taking'

Lucy Newlyn

Leave-taking

for Emma

The branches ripple
under the wind's caress
in their skimpy autumn dress,

as though their one thought
were nakedness, and a quick
wintry consummation.

Their loveliness is too light,
too eager – like a child
walking gladly for the first time

to school alone,
without so much as a wave,
or a backward look towards home.

But here *you* are: stepping
carefully down the stairs,
in your beautiful blue dress

and high-heeled shoes,
with your long hair smooth
and combed – pausing

as you enter your fourteenth year,
to leave me
wordless, standing there.

Time in a Bottle

Tonnie Walls

(extract from a novel)

Time in a Bottle

Bermuda's boys continued cleaning and cooking and taking care of her. It was only when they were at school that she had to fend for herself. But this day, she lacked the energy even to pour herself a bowl of cereal. She lay in bed looking at the clock, listening to its metallic ticks. 'How am I gone work tonight?' She was supposed to return to the factory on the late shift but there would be too many questions and besides, her arm was in a sling. She called the factory and told the foreman she needed more time off work. To her surprise, he didn't ask why. He told her that he understood and to take all the time she needed. Time, she reckoned that's what she needed, a little more time.

A mirror and a bottle of painkillers lay on the table next to her bed. She lifted the mirror and saw the face of a battered woman staring at her. Tears welled in her eyes but before she could cry there came a familiar knock at the front door. Instantly Bermuda reverted into stealth mode, but unable to glide out of bed to a more secure location she held still, not moving an inch lest the squeaking give her away. But she knew if the person looked inside, he or she could see her through the window. Holding the mirror to her breast she resigned to hold still and take her chances. The unexpected visitor knocked a few more times pausing between each series of knocks, possibly listening for movement inside the house. 'Go away, man!' Bermuda shouted in her mind. She eased her grip on the mirror's handle when she heard slow, deliberate steps walking along the rocks in the driveway away from the house. The visitor opened and closed his or her car door and finally drove away.

Bermuda rolled on her side and looked out her bedroom window. A neighbour, Peggy Winfry, was holding a rake while chatting with the visitor who hadn't gone very far after all. 'The insurance man!' Bermuda vented. 'I knew it was him.' Peggy pointed at Bermuda's house, shook her head, "no," and then the man drove off. 'Thank you, Peggy,' Bermuda whispered as her neighbour went back to raking leaves from her lawn. In Bermuda's own yard summer's emerald green grass had begun to fade to yellow and brown, hedges were beginning to shed, and a walnut tree which towered over her tiny house wore autumn's leaves like flowers on a hat. Bermuda remembered being a young girl in Mississippi, climbing trees much taller than the walnut in her front yard. After her wedding at the Justice of the Peace her father left her with Fidel and his family where she removed her mother's yellow maternity dress, slipped on Fidel's overalls and, against her sister-in-law's advice, went back to what she had been doing earlier that day -- climbing trees. On this occasion, however, she fell and landed in the back of Percy Black's truck. It was there that Junior was born and it was there that a sixteen year old Bermuda became mother. She longed to be sixteen again but without kids, without a husband, and without a shotgun wedding at the Justice of the Peace.

'Where did all the time go?' Bermuda asked herself. She was only thirty yet felt ten years older. Bermuda wanted to know how she could get back the lost years, how she could escape and start over. She returned the mirror to the table, knocking over her bottle of painkillers and, suddenly, she had her answer. Bermuda lifted the bottle and knew this was the path to freedom. She went to the kitchen for a glass of water. On the way back she stopped and looked into her sons' rooms. She half smiled at their attempt to make their beds. Underneath the covers bunched-up sheets betrayed their efforts. Bermuda lifted the covers and with her good arm made their beds properly and smoothed the top layer. 'I have to say goodbye to my babies.' The sound of her voice surprised her. It was that of a woman much older than thirty. What does one write in a suicide letter, she wondered. She had thought to kill herself when she was a girl. Her mother, Katherine, had found in the shed a love letter that she had written but not yet sent to Elvis Presley. When night came, Bermuda's mother insisted that she bathe before going to bed. And just before she could dry herself, Katherine entered the room and beat her with an extension cord. Bermuda couldn't decide who she wanted to kill more -- herself or her mother but she was certain that she wanted to die. And had she had a bottle of take-me-heaven or something she was sure she would have ended her life. Skin cut and etched with wilts she cried herself to sleep. The next morning Katherine prepared a big breakfast just for Bermuda. She had rolled dough and, with a cup, cut them into biscuits. She scrambled eggs and fried thick slices of rind bacon just the way Bermuda liked it. 'De Lawd told me to beat you, gal,' her mother said. 'Donchu know dey'll kill you for sending love letters to a white man?' Bermuda saw no point in jeopardising a good meal, and so, didn't answer. 'Now you recite de 23rd Psalm and then eat yo' breakfast.' While she listened to her daughter recite David's Psalm, Katherine cut the biscuits in half. Bermuda's mouth watered and, as steam rose from the hot layers, Bermuda prayed faster. 'Slow down, gal! Don't rush de Lawd.' Bermuda did as she was told and watched her mother open a special jar of homemade jam that she had been saving for winter. She spread butter and jam on the biscuits and then handed her daughter a cup of milk that she had gotten from their cow herself. Bermuda was perplexed by her mother's exceptionally kind manner and couldn't believe she was the same woman who just the night before had nearly beat her to death. Bermuda enjoyed her special breakfast, then went off to school and, until this autumn morning, never thought again about killing herself.

Bermuda decided to write a letter to her three sons. She searched for a pen and a clean sheet of paper but could only find a pencil and a paper grocery bag. She tore the paper as neatly as she could, climbed into bed and began writing.

> *To My Dear Sons,*
> *I'm sorry to leave you like this, especially since you're all so young. But you're big boys and I know you can take care of yourselves. And, I know Theola and my family will look after you. When you're older I hope you'll understand that this is something I had to do. Promise me you'll be good boys. And, Junior, make sure you teach your brothers the 23rd Psalm. Until we're together again.*
> *Love,*
> *Mom*
> *PS. Don't forget to rake the leaves.*

Fidel grew tired of the motel and so spent the night on an old cot that one of the workers at some point had dragged into his club. But one end of the cot smelled like pee and the other like mothballs, so he spent the whole night tossing and turning between pee and mothballs. When he had had enough he got up and turned the mattress over, which helped if only marginally. But the cot squeaked. Every time he rolled one way or the other, which he had the habit of doing, he would wake up. Finally, he put a bottle of Wild Turkey to his lips, drank as much as he could, and sleep came. But an hour or two later, the autumn sun peered through the window and Fidel's eyes opened. His ashy legs and feet reached for slippers as he sat up in bed. He rubbed his back which ached because of the cot or perhaps from years of driving trucks. He was glad to have given it up. A million miles he drove for Jordan Transports. He probably drove a million more miles, he guessed, on vacations and visiting relatives in Mississippi. He was glad to be away from the south, away from picking cotton, milking cows, and slopping hogs.

Fidel thought heard something outside. He slid his feet deeper into his slippers, got up, and stumbled to the window. Fall had come. All around, he saw brightly coloured leaves on trees against a background of clear blue sky. He spotted the intruder. It was a horse, a streak of white amidst the blinding colours. It ran back and forth across the lawn and then vanished. 'Can't be no horse,' Fidel told himself. 'Gotta be Wild Turkey.' But then he heard a noise out front, something banging against metal. Fidel walked past the bar and pool table then peered out the window where he saw the horse kicking his car. 'What the hell? Is you crazy?' Fidel shouted. Heat rose in his chest and for reasons that he could not explain, he grabbed his keys and ran for the car. When Fidel burst from the door the horse trotted down the long driveway then turned and looked at Fidel from the road. 'You is crazy!' Fidel huffed. 'But you 'bout to be dead and crazy!' Fidel started the car, revved up the engine a couple of times, and went after the horse who was in far better shape than the Buick which, old now and not warmed up enough for a chase, squealed and jerked its way along State Street. Fidel did the best he could to keep up, ignoring stop lights, stop signs, and dodging potholes along the way. It wasn't long before the police were after him. Their sirens roared and they summoned Fidel to pull over. But he had to catch that horse, so he ignored them and forged ahead. One officer pointed a gun from his window and fired.

Bermuda placed the letter on the table and caught a glimpse of her reflection in the mirror. 'I can't go like dis.' She went to the bathroom and filled a bath with extra baby oil and bubbles. After her bath, she went to the kitchen, turned on the stove, and put her straightening comb and curling iron on a low flame. 'I gotta do something with dis hair. It was hard to straighten her hair, given that one shoulder was still healing, but she was determined not to be found with a 'nappy head.' So, with a regular comb, she began the painful process of combing and parting her hair. On the scalp where the hair was parted she applied Posner oil and worked it in along the short lengths of hair which sizzled when she applied the hot, metal comb. She burned her ear a couple of times but continued and when the hair was all straightened she took the curling iron from the flame and curled her hair. And the back, which was too short to curl, she slicked down with hair gel. At her vanity, she applied Fashion Fair makeup and painted her lips brown. 'Alex likes me with brown lips,' she said. Her face done, she went to the closet and looked for a nice dress. 'This will have to do.' She removed a white dress from its hanger. 'Not as nice as my other white one but Fidel done tore that one up.' She stepped into the dress, worked it up her body but, because of her shoulder, could not manage to fasten it in the back. She sprayed herself with Charlie perfume but made no attempt to do her nails. There was one thing left to do. The bottle of painkillers was on the table. Next to it was the glass of water. How clear it was, she thought, as clear as her life was muddy. She opened the bottle, swallowed half the pills, and washed them down with water. She swallowed the other half, washed it down, and lay down in bed. Bermuda closed her eyes and felt her heart beat. She hoped there was no Hell and if there was she hoped God wouldn't send her there.

The bullet hit its target. Fidel's rear white-walled tire exploded and the designer hubcap went flying. But Fidel kept going. This time the officer aimed higher. The back of Fidel's head was in sight. The officer fired, shattering Fidel's rear window, forcing the police car to veer and dodge the glass. But Fidel forged ahead, following the horse as it turned left at Clark Gas Station. Together, they raced down the hill into a neighbourhood passing people who were, of course, shocked to see a horse being chased by an aging, once fashionable Buick, which was being pursued by the police. Fidel followed closely but when the horse jumped over a white picket fence Fidel was unable to react quickly enough and tore right through the yard, the fence, and a large but neat pile of raked leaves. The A-frame broke and the front of the car collapsed to the ground bringing it to a halt. When the dust cleared, Fidel saw the horse standing in front of a small house on 70th Street and, at once, Fidel understood why he hadn't been able to sleep. He ran from the car and, with two policemen at his heels, he burst in the front door. The policemen grabbed him and wrestled him to the ground but he broke away, ran for the bedroom where he saw a woman sleeping, and he screamed her name, 'Bermuda!'

Fidel rode in the ambulance with Bermuda and spent the night with her in the hospital. The next day Patient Moore, as Bermuda was called, was sent to spend the next four weeks at the Alton Mental Health Centre. Her uncle, whom Fidel had called, decided that the boys would stay with him and his wife in St. Louis. Fidel felt responsible for the whole thing and did not challenge them. With a heavy heart, he watched as his wife and sons were taken away from him.

Fidel returned to sleeping in the motel by day and working in his club by night. He thought to move back into the house he once shared with Bermuda but for some reason or another he decided not to. Instead, he drove by there each day and peered through the windows in search of light, movement, noise, anything that resembled the life he once had. Days and weeks went by without any news from his family. Winter came early. Fidel brushed the snow from his leather jacket as he walked into a crowded restaurant on State Street and ordered take-away. The aromas of basted ham and smoked turkey danced around him. People laughed, sipped eggnog, and stuffed themselves with helpings of collard greens, dressing, peach cobbler, and sweet potato pie. It was Thanksgiving, a feast bigger than Christmas. Fidel looked at all the happy people around him -- families, spouses, and children then took his meal in two aluminium containers and slipped out into the night. He parked his car in his and Bermuda's driveway, popped in an 8-track and as Barry White sang 'Never Gonna Give You Up,' Fidel cried in front of the empty, lifeless house. When the song ended, Fidel opened one of the food containers. In it he found salt crackers and thick slices of hog head cheese. If this didn't make him happy, it did make him less sad. He dried his tears and began eating his Thanksgiving dinner.

Bermuda and her boys celebrated Thanksgiving with her uncle, his wife, and a host of relatives who came all the way from Mississippi to be with her. Her mother and sisters cooked a soul food feast which was highlighted by 'chitlins' and deep fried turkey. The next day, Bermuda's family went south while she and her boys went east and, after a month in the care of others, they returned to their home and took care of each other. Her boys did not know where she had gone or why, and for some reason they knew not to ask. They were happy to be together again and to be home. Following their great uncle's advice Junior, Tyrone, and Alex behaved themselves. They continued cooking and cleaning and looking after their mother until a day much like the one on which they were separated they went back to school. It was on that day that

Bermuda first received what she described as 'nice' visits from Fidel. He came wearing his best clothes and was scented in Aramis. He brought gifts and made promises. He kissed and massaged his wife in places she swore he hadn't touched in years. And then one afternoon as they lay in bed he asked, 'Can I come back home?' She said she would think about it. Weeks passed. But the longer she thought about it the shorter, less frequent, and less romantic his visits became. He stopped bringing gifts and promises. He stopped wearing his best clothes. And his Aramis cologne was replaced by booze and later by the scent of other women. And during his last visit he entered the house without knocking. 'Made up yo' mind yet? he asked. And when she answered, 'No,' their rekindled honeymoon was over. Fidel walked to the front door then tuned around and gave Bermuda a look that made her step back against the wall. 'Dis my house,' he said. 'And if you don't get out I'm a burn it down.'

Gardening

Colm O'Shea

GARDENING

(Extract from a full-length screenplay)

FADE IN:

EXT. WEB-SCAPE -- CONTINUOUS

A hyper-vivid landscape: a city overgrown with jungle. The synthetic sky crackles - electric storm.

A heavily-muscled monster hunkers on a decaying car's roof, one of many long-deserted in ancient gridlock.

The creature's eyes blaze. Suddenly he explodes from his perch, leaping from car to car, the epitome of animal power, all force and focus.

His run intensifies, leaping now from building to building. He climbs a skyscraper, vines twisting up the length - an amazing display of athletic prowess.

Panting at the summit, he surveys the empty metropolis. He roars at the sky, rejoicing in his raw power.

BUTLER, a tiny rabbit butler, peeks from the foliage, clears his throat. The monster growls, glares down.

> BUTLER
> (hopping back)
> Beg pardon, sir. It is teatime. May I suggest a brief break, maybe some refreshment?

INT. AL'S FLAT

Spartan room, no window, neighbour's aggressive music muffled by the wall.

AL, (early 20s, emaciated) reclines on a lounge chair. His "halo" (a thin neon hair-band arc) glows pale blue in the dusk - then suddenly darkens.

Al sharply inhales, opens his eyes. He is attached to a glucose/micro-nutrient drip. Squinting, his eyes trace the IV to find the bag is near empty.

He fumbles in a box by his side, finds a final fresh bag, replaces the empty one which he throws on the ground near a pile of empties. He sits back, shuts his eyes. The halo lights again.

Al twitches, re-entering his virtual-world. A reflex sigh of pleasure, then he is still as a corpse.

EXT. WEB-SCAPE - SKYSCRAPER ROOFTOP -- CONTINUOUS

Al/monster flexes his muscles.

> BUTLER
> Welcome back, sir. May I say, that was quite a brief dining experience. Have you partaken of enough roughage today? The human colon requires a certain amount of-

Al flattens Butler with his fist - the icon vanishes.

Al/monster contemplates the dizzying drop to the street below. The wind whistles.

He paces back from the brink, prep for a running start. He charges, leaps, plummets.

Asphalt rushes to meet him - he falls headfirst, a dart.

Butler, tiny wings flapping on his back, circles his master in descent, notebook and pen at the ready.

> BUTLER
> Pardon me, Mr. Al. You need to leave now if you want to make your night shift.

INT. AL'S FLAT

Al sits up, reluctantly regards his nurse's uniform.

INT. NURSING HOME FOYER - NIGHT

Al clocks in, passes his supervisor tapping his watch.

INT. NURSING HOME - CONTINUOUS

Al washes haloed clients, changes drips, colostomy bags. He is dispassionate, as if servicing flimsy machines.

INT. PRIVATE ROOM - NIGHT

Al changes an old man's IV. The man's halo darkens. He wakes, a hunted look on his face, grips Al.

                          AL
              Just changing your feed, sir. All's well.

The man mouths something. Al bends to hear. The man dies. Al checks for a pulse. About to hit the alert, he stops.

Al checks corridor, closes the door. He pockets an IV bag, sits on a chair. He puts the halo on, shuts his eyes.

INT. PRIVATE WARD - LATER

Blinking into Al's POV: Al's supervisor stands over him, two orderlies remove the corpse on a gurney.

                          SUPERVISOR
              Back in the land of the living.

                          AL
                    (removing halo)
              Uh, he was already-

                          SUPERVISOR
                    (exiting)
              Hand in your ID to security.

Al regards the halo in his hands.

INT. AL'S APT - LATER

Al enters. He peels off his uniform, stands still in the room. We see every sinew of his hollowed form.

The neighbour's muffled aggressive music starts up.

> AL
> (suddenly furious)
> SHUT *UP!!*

EXT. WEB-SCAPE - SKYSCRAPER ROOFTOP -- CONTINUOUS

As before, Al/monster plummets to the street below. Butler circles his falling master, notebook in hand.

> BUTLER
> Pardon me, Mr. Al. A Mr. Zeke called.

Al roars. He grabs Butler's foot. Butler hovers patiently, Al hangs from the furry white paw.

> AL
> What does he want?

> BUTLER
> He neglected to mention.

> AL
> Well is it *important*?

> BUTLER
> I wouldn't presume to say, sir.

> AL
> (resigned)
> Take me.

Butler swings Al like a throwing hammer. Al rockets through the liquid window of a nearby building into -

INT. WEB-SCAPE -- NIGHTCLUB

Elegant aliens and cartoon animals mingle with humans. Breakdancers perform on a *Saturday Night Fever*-style floor which, Escher-like, is vertical and horizontal. Al/monster crashes into a booth where Zeke (human) sits nursing a multicolour milkshake.

>   ZEKE
>   Hey Al, wanna milkshake?

>   AL
>   What do you want, Zeke?

>   ZEKE
>   Is that any way to greet a friend?

>   AL
>   You're my brother's friend.

>   ZEKE
>   You should cocoon your profile if you don't want to
>   be disturbed.

>   AL
>   Can't cocoon. Blacked out last month.   Insurance
>   won't cover it.
>   (beat)
>   What can I say? This is the closest I can legally
>   get to being friendless.

>   ZEKE
>   You've got a halo problem when God tells you you
>   need to socialize more.

They sit in silence, Al hulking inside the booth.

>   ZEKE
>   You might want to...

Al remembers his form, morphs down to human: a healthier-
looking version of his real body.

>   ZEKE
>   Wanna milkshake?

>   AL
>   What flavour is that?

                        ZEKE
        Birthday.
                      (sips)
        It's pretty good.

                        AL
        Don't like *Birthdays*. Bad aftertaste. Had a
        Homecoming once. It was okay.

Several breakdancers defy gravity. Zeke nods at them.

                        ZEKE
        Quadriplegics. I checked the log - they almost
        never leave the floor.

                        AL
        God assigned me a butler.

Butler hops onto the table, Zeke scratches Butler's ear.
Butler shuts his eyes, happily foot-thumps the table.

A complex PUZZLE CUBE manifests in Zeke's hands.

                     PUZZLE CUBE
               (low tones, background noise)
        Anyone-for-puzzle-cube?

Zeke plays, eyes on the cube, fingers a blur.

                        AL
        Thing won't leave me be. Keeps asking if I'm
        lonely. Gives me dietary advice!

Zeke laughs.

                     PUZZLE CUBE
        Level 2: Hey-you're-not-bad!

                        AL
        It's not a laughing matter. He's started advising
        I "wake" every twenty hours, to eat and get REM
        sleep.

                        ZEKE
        You're kidding.

                                                    197

                        AL
    It's a psych program. Long-eared little rat.
    Never comes right out and *says* anything. Always a
    suggestion.

                    PUZZLE CUBE
    Level 3: Wow-not-just-a-pretty-face!

                        AL
    I was in the middle of some deep stuff last week.
    Out of the blue, it suggests I just... Wake.
    *"Why not do some jumping jacks with a family
    member or school chum?"*

                        ZEKE
    Jumping jacks?
                    (to Butler)
    Was that your idea?

Butler nods enthusiastically.

                    PUZZLE CUBE
    Level 4: Lock-up-your-daughters-this-guy's-on-fire!

                        AL
    No one should tell you to Wake.
                    (to Butler)
    It's unconstitutional.

Butler lowers his ears, cowers.

                        ZEKE
    God has to cover its ass.

                        AL
    Yeah well… If I make my minimum chow-and-sleep
    breaks over the next six months they'll let me get
    back to my privacy.

                    PUZZLE CUBE
    Level 5: They-should-patent-your-DNA!

                        ZEKE
    So. Do you want a milk-

                          AL
          No, Zeke.

Al slaps Zeke's Puzzle Cube closed.

                     PUZZLE CUBE
          Gameovergameovergameover-yousuuuuuck-

Cube disintegrates. Butler looks anxiously from Al to Zeke.

                          AL
          I don't want to call a school chum, I don't want
          to do any jumping jacks, and I definitely don't
          want a goddamn milkshake. Why did you call me?

                         ZEKE
          I just wanted to ask you a question.
                              (beat)
          Want to live forever?

Al glowers.

                         ZEKE
          If I told you could stay lit up all the time - no
          more waking - would you be interested?

Two obnoxiously exaggerated SEX DRONES slink into the
booth, puncturing the tension.

                      SEX DRONES
          Hey there. Don't you STUDS want to chat with REAL
          WOMEN about your DEEPEST FANTASIES?

They stuff their over-sized cleavage in the men's faces.

                      SEX DRONES
          GIVE IN! GIVE IN TO WHAT YOU NEED!

                          AL
          Butler! Deal with these… things.

                        BUTLER
          Without delay. Ladies, follow me please.

He hops away. Drones follow his cottontail, mesmerized.

                         SEX DRONES
                         (to Butler)
             Hey there, STUD. Wanna chat with REAL WOMEN
             about...

                            AL
             We can't talk here. C'mon.

They dive into the dance floor. It gives way like water.

(*They manifest in a cave.*)

                           ZEKE
             It'll take the butler time to burrow here.

Zeke produces a stick with a marshmallow on it. A fire
lights between the men.

                           ZEKE
             Let's get nostalgic.

They roast marshmallows. The fire crackles. Al bites his
mallow - his mouth briefly pixilates.

                            AL
             Woah. These are strong.

                           ZEKE
             They get stronger. Go slow.
                           (beat)
             I need to find your brother. I can't think of
             anyone else who knows him.

                            AL
             No one knows Yogi. Not really.

The marshmallows grow into psychedelic-geometric flames.

                           ZEKE
             You two are so alike.

                            AL
             Don't say that.

ZEKE
It's true. They slapped a butler on him too. Did
you know that?

Al shakes his head.

ZEKE
Two blackouts in one week. And lo - the clouds
part, God assigns him a Cheshire Cat. Not a
friendly monitor like your rabbit. *This* was a
psych program. Yogi *hated* that thing. Really got
in his head.

Zeke's marshmallow pattern briefly forms a cat's face.

AL
What's this got to do with staying lit up all the
time?

ZEKE
Yogi vanished months ago. I finally tracked his
butler down in the crystal forest. I broke off a
flake to view the last seconds of his log.

AL
And?

ZEKE
The butler's log for the last zero-point-three
seconds it was in contact with Yogi runs to over
seventy experiential hours. Garbled… madness.

Al bites his mallow, preoccupied.

AL
So? Yogi's butler broke. I need to go.

ZEKE
Wait. I don't think the cat's memory is faulty.
Before the university cancelled our funding,
Yogi and I were working on sensory array stuff.
Cognitive amplification. Temporal distortion.

Gardening

> AL
>
> What's temporal distortion?

> ZEKE
>
> We're snails.

> AL
>
> You and me?

> ZEKE
>
> Everyone. Human minds are like snails. We've got synapse technology now and we can record, share, synthesize experiences and blah blah, but, y'know, we're basically the same neurotic cretins we were a hundred thousand years ago.

> AL
>
> Snails.

> ZEKE
>
> Yeah. We crawl through time at more or less the same rate, meet, rub our antennae together. I was trying to become a faster snail. Crawl quicker, munch more info, grow longer antennae into the web. But Yogi turned into something completely different. A lightning bolt.

> AL
>
> You've lost me.

> ZEKE
>
> Well, he lost me too. He lost all of us.
> (beat)
> *The primal speed limit*. That's what he called it. Our ancient lizard brain. Holds us back, like a vast anchor. Roots us to time. Yogi wanted a new halo interface, something to cut the anchor. He called it "The Crown."

The two mallow flames fuse to one complex pattern, growing between the men. They bite it like candyfloss.

> AL
>
> The Crown? How does it work?

                    ZEKE
          It didn't. Two test subjects had psychotic breaks.

The psychedelic flame becomes a screaming head.

                    ZEKE
          We were shelved. A liability. But now, with the
          time disparity in the cat's records...

                    AL
          You think Yogi pulled it off. Cutting this ancient
          root, this anchor. What's it mean?

                    ZEKE
          Well, in theory, the crown could speed
          consciousness *billions* of times past the primal
          speed limit. An instant in our time would be eons
          to a crown-user. He'd have, for all intents and
          purposes… eternal life.

The pattern unfolds, becomes all background space now, a
dazzling geometric infinity.

                    AL
          Eternal life. Are you saying… Yogi might have
          found a key to heaven?

                    ZEKE
          I don't know. He could be a vegetable right now,
          fried out of his brainpan.

The men slowly break into simpler geometric forms.

                    ZEKE
          Either way, he never has to Wake again to take a
          piss and change his feed-bag.

The simplified avatars dissolve into geometric infinity.

                    ZEKE (V.O.)
                (voice becoming synthetic)
          Help me learn if Yogi's dead, or a god. Wanna
          take a trip in the Wake?

                         AL (V.O.)
        I'm not ready… to get into that right now.

                        ZEKE (V.O.)
        Dwell on it. Take all the time… you need.

The geometric pattern condenses into a crystal shard.

INT. SUBTERRANEAN MARKET - DAY

Ramshackle stalls sell everything: microchips to herbs.
All signs are visual, no words. Al squeezes through the
throng, stops at an open half-door.

A young Chinese boy pokes his head out.

                           AL
                      (in Mandarin)
        A box of 25 - no, make that 50 feed bags. Put it
        on my tab.

The boy disappears. Al waits, tired and drawn. The boy
reappears, hands a large box to Al.

                           AL
        Hey! These are just glucose.

                          BOY
        Good. Glucose. Good for energy.

                           AL
        No. I need multi-nutrient and glucose. *Multi-
        nutrient.*

The boy reluctantly takes the box, vanishes.

                           AL
        And throw in some fibre sachets.

A decrepit flower-seller offers her last wilting flower. She
continues holding it out, he keeps refusing.
She puts the flower in his hand and walks off.

                           AL
        What am I supposed to do with this?

The boy returns with a much smaller box.

> BOY
> Multi-feed's gone up. This all your credit's good
> for.

Al considers the pathetic volume.

> BOY
> Take or leave! Busy!

INT. AL'S FLAT

Al opens his small feed box. Resting on the drip bags
is the rotting flower. He puts it in an improvised vase,
reclines on his lounger.

EXT. WEB-SCAPE -- BEACH -- MORNING

An infinite strand. Al sits alone. Surf rumbles. Butler
burrows out of the sand, shakes a crab from his long ear.

> BUTLER
> Some *real* sunlight would help your body produce
> Vitamin D, essential for preventing rickets. And
> helpful for avoiding certain forms of cancer,
> depression, and even - some experts believe -
> schizophrenia.

Waves crash.

> AL
> Maybe it's time I took some sun.

Butler perks, rocks on his feet, fiddles with his tie.

INT. BATHROOM - MORNING

Al scrubs and coughs in the cramped shower.

INT. FLAT - DAY

Al sits, clothed, bored. He twirls the woman's flower in
his hand. A train of ants troop around his foot.

MOMENTS LATER

Down on all-fours, Al follows the ant train to his new box
of feed bags. He removes a leaking, encrusted bag. It is
covered with ants.

INT. AL'S FLAT

Al sits at his desk, staring at an antique rotary phone.
Finally he dials. It rings a long time. Zeke answers.

                         AL
             Zeke? Al. Count me in.

A small device prints out a piece of paper.

                         ZEKE (O.S.)
             Outstanding. That's my Wake address. We'll hit
             the road first thing tomorrow.

Al viciously stamps down on something several times.

                         AL
             I have ants.

                         ZEKE (O.S.)
             Nobody's perfect. See you soon.
                   (dial tone)

Al keeps staring down. The muffled aggressive music from
next door starts up.

The Initiation

Jesselynn Sutanto

The Initiation

Chapter One: 'Agility'

Elder Baru was relatively young for an Elder. Delima placed him somewhere in his late twenties; old enough to have a respectable number of years under his belt as an Active, young enough to set off an attack of giggles among the girls each time he gave his lazy smile.

'Welcome to Agility Ten. I trust that by now, your Elders have told you time and again how dangerous an Assassin's life is. But just to illustrate exactly how... painful a single mistake can be...'

Elder Baru removed his left glove and waggled two stumps on his hand where his index finger and thumb used to be. New skin had grown to cover the wounds, but his hand was still mangled enough to make Delima nauseous. He smiled grimly at the gasps of horror.

'The target had set up a line of defences. I'd managed to Disarm most of them, but as you can see, I failed to see the last one. A Fire Bombe.'

He replaced his leather glove and tapped on his left leg with his wooden cane. *Thunk.* The noise managed to slice through the murmurs of the autumn wind and the rustling of the drying leaves. Several of the girls, moments ago perched eagerly at the front of the group, lowered their eyes and huddled closer together, wary of the Elder but unwilling to edge closer to the border of the Darke Woode.

Elder Baru raised his eyebrow and gave yet another grin. There was no giggling this time. Keeping his gaze on their eyes, he lifted the hem of his left trouser and showed a wooden stump.

A terrible silence fell over each Disciple. Elder Baru nodded at the class of sixteen, not missing the way that the group had subconsciously shuffled into a tighter huddle.

'It might not seem like it to you, but I was extremely lucky to only lose a leg and two fingers. I couldn't go on as an Active, of course, but the Council allowed me back in Tchu-Ay as an Elder to teach the Year Ten

Disciples.' He chuckled to himself. 'Yes, yes, I know. The irony of it: a cripple teaching Agility Ten. But the Council has its reasons, and who are we to question them? Perhaps they assigned me to this particular class because in my year, I was the only one to receive full marks in Agility. Perhaps they simply wanted me to serve as... an example.'

This time, even the boys took a step away from the Elder. But not Delima. She stayed rooted to the spot, forgetting even to blink. Elder Baru was a personification of her fears, a preview of herself ten years to come. If I pass my Initiation, that is, she thought bitterly.

As if hearing her thoughts, Elder Baru's eyes locked on hers.

'This is your last year as a Disciple. In less than a year you will be undergoing your Initiation. Some of you will fail. You are the lucky ones. You'll become an Inactive and go through life without any wants or worries.'

Several of the cockier Disciples snorted, but at a turn of Elder Baru's head, they all fell silent once more.

'Think you're too good for life as an Inactive, do you?' He shrugged. 'Well, you are. Inactives are nothing more than parasites, feeding off the wealth that the Actives and Elders risk their lives earning every single day. But what's the alternative to becoming an Inactive? Let's see— Ah, you *could* lose your life during your Initiation.'

The pairs of eyes in front of him widened.

'Yes, you could lose your life during your Initiation. Very easily, in fact. The Council has designed the Initiation such that, in the unlikely event that you pass, there can be no doubt whatsoever that you are ready to be stationed as an Active.'

Despite his wooden leg, Elder Baru moved about with the natural grace of a cat. He walked around the Disciples, eyeing them up and down and making them huddle even closer to one another.

'So yes, because of its nature, death is very much a part of the Initiation,' he said.

Did he just look at me? Delima thought. She snapped her eyes around, but Elder Baru had already walked past her and she could only see his back. Nonetheless, she made sure to blast his retreating back with a few silent curses.

'The few of you who manage to not only survive the Initiation, but also fulfil the requirements of your individual task, will begin a new life as an Active. What an honour that will be!'

He came to a halt in front of the class.

'But what does honour give you? Only arrogance, which will ultimately lead to carelessness. And when you get careless, you are immediately relieved of your Active status and carted back to Tchu-Ay... in a body bag. Or you could get lucky and end up a cripple like me.' Elder Baru smiled.

Silence greeted the end of his speech.

'So this is the one piece of advice I find worth giving you,' he said. 'Don't make mistakes.'

Sixteen pairs of eyes, round with fear, stared back at him. Satisfied, he clapped his hands together, making a few of the students jump.

'Enough of the long faces,' he called out. 'Warm ups! Five laps around the village, extended strides, complete silence. I don't want to hear your feet thumping on the ground, no huffing and gasping for breath, *complete silence*. End at the edge of Darke Woode. Go!'

Delima glanced around the crowd of fellow Disciples, looking for her friend Miana. Despite the fact that their traditional soot-coloured uniform only allowed the wearer's eyes to show, it wasn't difficult to pick out the tall, slender figure elbowing everyone out of the way. And oh yes – Delima rolled her eyes – there was Miana, in the lead and pulling away fast.

The rest of the group was pulling away fast too, away from Delima.

Being the shortest person in her year must have some advantages, she thought. She just hadn't had the chance to discover what they were yet.

By the time she reached the turn at the blacksmith's forge, Miana was already out of sight and the others soon would be.

She noticed Old Blacksmith stepping out of his shop to have a smoke. Oh wonderful, that was all she needed; for Old Blacksmith to see them doing laps. Now every Inactive in the village was going to step outside and enjoy watching her failing her Agility class yet again. Old Blacksmith grinned at her, his hand-rolled cigarette dangling nastily from his blackened teeth.

'Laps, eh, missy?'

Even his voice sounded like a leer.

He couldn't be outright rude to her. Technically, as an Inactive, he wasn't even supposed to say anything to her, save for 'Mornin' miss' or 'Evenin' miss' or 'How sharp do ye want this blade, miss?' But he knew Delima was shy. He knew she wouldn't say anything to the Elders. They all knew it, and they didn't hesitate to push her.

She ignored him and ran faster. As a result, by the time she was on her third round, she was already out of breath.

Six miles down, she consoled herself, four more to go.

And there was Sho the Dressmaker with her Apprentice, waiting outside their shop.

News certainly gets around fast amongst the Inactives, Delima thought bitterly, at least faster than I can run.

She looked away, but not before she caught their mocking grins. Focus on something else, she told herself, focus on… oh, the buildings, why not?

She sighed. She was running along Tradesmen Hill now, and the buildings around her were not exactly a sight for tired eyes. Made of cheap Dandyrose wood, the trade shops had been built with the least amount of effort and thought.

She didn't know much about how Tchu-Ay came to be as it was. Nobody knew when the town split in two, the strong group, the Elders, Disciples and Actives, and the rest. The strong lived in the Inner Ring, which took up all the ground that was nicely level. The rest were the Inactives, the ones who had failed their Initiation, and lived in the poorer quarters. They were mostly tradesmen and farmers, and built their homes anywhere they wanted. Not on the level land, of course, they built on the rock cliffs and hills that flanked the north-western side of the Inner Ring and the Darke Woode which stretched for miles on the eastern side.

The first Inactives had hollowed out parts of the rock cliffs that flanked the western border and eked out a meagre survival, while the Inner Ring flourished and sprouted imposing structures, complete with a stone wall segregating it from the Outer Ring. Over the years, the Inactives had added to their caves so that now they had proper wooden buildings that ended as a cave at the back. As the population of Inactives increased, they expanded upwards as well, flanking each house with sturdy beams that supported the house above it. Narrow trails snaked between the hillside houses. It was these trails that the Disciples were often asked to run along.

'Really, it's quite the ideal situation,' Miana had surmised a few weeks ago as they walked past the hillside shops, collecting items in preparation for the start of their last year as Disciples.

'I mean, they don't even have to work. The Actives are the ones who bring in the money. All the Inactives ever have to do is learn how to sew or cut wood. Such an idyllic life, don't you think?'

Delima had nodded her agreement.

'There are so many of them, though,' Miana continued. 'You'd think that they'd learn to build wider streets! Why can't they learn from the Inner Ring?'

The Inner Ring, with its five granite monoliths – the House of Disciples, the House of Discipline, the House of Elders, the Foreign Offices, where all visitors had to report before coming in and out of the Inner Ring, and the House of the Council.

Each building was huge and decadent, and spaced far enough from one another as to allow a generous dose of sunlight each day. The streets in the Inner Ring were so wide that several trade shops could fit into any one of them with room to spare.

At the time, Delima had deferred to the inflexion of absolute certainty in Miana's voice and agreed that yes, aren't the Inactives just plain backward? But lately she could not help wondering if the haphazard layout of their streets had more to do with the fact that the thousands of Inactives that made up more than nine-tenths of the population were limited to about a tenth of the land.

Delima hated having such thoughts. They made life so problematic, and what with her being naturally multi-untalented, she really did not need any more complications.

So, it was with great relief that she finished her final lap and veered east towards the Darke Woode. She didn't have to look back to know that the Inactives were all peering out of their ramshackle doorways and windows, watching her retreating back. Each step took her further from that baleful, hungry look that the Inactives always gave them, and by the time she reached the border of the forest, she was feeling almost optimistic.

She caught up with the rest of the class just as Elder Baru was wrapping up his instructions. She shuffled into the group of Disciples, grateful for the anonymity that her uniform gave her. She looked around for Miana's familiar lanky frame and darting eyes and made her way to her friend.

'There you are!' Miana whispered as Delima sidled over.

'What're we supposed to be doing?'

'Tree-climbing,' Miana said. She gestured subtly at the Dark Woode. 'We're doing Smooth Pinedusts today, Grappling Hooks Number Twelve.'

Delima gave a soft groan.

'The mind is an octopus'

Deborah Mason

The mind is an octopus

whose long tentacles writhe out
to grab each floating thought
and pull it in to coherence.

So a small vague longing,
sculling slowly past, is hauled in
to be examined with rigour.

But that's a mistake.
The octopus hasn't thought this through.

For this erotic longing,
happy to laze in the shallows,
flounders when dragged in too deeply.

It kicks the octopus hard in the head,
crushing rational thoughts, bursting open
the floodgates to overwhelming passion.

The octopus flails, moans and is engulfed.

'The Music'

Roy Davids

The Music

                  slowly lifts its head
from the middle of the orchestra;
silently commanding, eyes half closed.
Temples tighten. Mouths go dry.
The air focuses like a buddha,
ready to receive its votaries.

The orchestra sways to its partner's
lead and together they enter the dance.
Music can lift and fall like wind,
sweep across landscapes, fondle
fields, lick along the lines of bays,
filter the sea through its fingertips.

Or sit gossiping on a wall.
Wise, it will philosophise,
nag at a single tone or theme.
Brash, it is a hurdy gurdy band.
Gentle, it can slip into a waltz.
Sad, it turns away, and weeps.

I like music that wants to press
my cheek against its shoulder,
music so affectively refined,
it seems like water falling.
High on this side of silence,
made from a skein of sighs.

Poems

Aaron Rench

The Story Never Sleeps

1.

A sequence of events is all
she asks, something gripping
with an underdog attached,

every night before the prayers,
the polishing of teeth
and the closing of eyes.

I will learn to tell the story
for the dreams: the difference
is night and day—the way

they chase each other mad
as skylarks in the library
of her smallest years.

I am a lucky witness
to the backyard myth—
the shape she gives a tale.

2.

The outdoor circuit of home
is rife with her mosey
and I follow, leaving space

just to see what might
become of the plot
that she is thickening.

She eyes a rocky path,
selects that route then
disappears around

the corner of the house,
the corner of a dream.
In the end there is

a fable that she follows
through the trees, the forest,
leading to the door.

3.

In a story she has
heard, a giant meets
a shepherd for a duel.

David left the armor
with the king, took river
stones to kill Goliath.

She asks to have it told
every night for a time
as though she is trying to learn,

going back to practice,
some important thing.
On this occasion

she comes inside a little
heavier than when she left.
The burden goes unnoticed

until she is sleeping and I
hang her coat, its pockets
clap with the smack of stones.

Letter to a Future Widow

What did we do with the time when
there was no need to push the pen?
That's now lost, but we can win
    back with these words,
and try to capture could-have-beens
    though voice is unheard.

But still, it's hard to fit this love
on a page, as we prepare to shove
off for good. Though one won't move
    the other will depart,
dividing hand from perfect glove,
    clinching us apart.

And since we cannot reunite,
look straight into the eye of night
until we seem so close, so tight
    from final embrace
that the hand reaching for your sight,
    must let the writing cease.

Palouse Farm Sonnet

I.

Soon they'll burn these fields into acres
of ash and leave behind the charred hills,
the wheat scars, grain soot and stubbled lentils.
But with its back left broken a land still stirs.
This body of earth, its given ghost blurs
the roads around these farms where hay spills.
Where tractors carved the ground now a fog fills
the valleys in channeled foam wonder.
A landscape of repeating parabolas
made of dirt, loam and gravel; it will haunt
a visitor down every other road
they ever travel. Even if there was
a way to block it out there'd be a taunt
buried in the memory like a goad.

Palouse Farm Sonnet

II.

Here there is no waiting; it comes to us.
The winter turns this patch into rolling
little polar caps, the harvest dust
frozen in, clamped to the cold, loose tillings.
The barn red blooming in a field of snow,
the wounded frost still strobing white and silver
as sun and moon push their various glows.
Never did a place bear the weight of stars
like this: a local magnificence, the sky
nearly spending its worth in one place
a small theater, with cheap tickets, empty
seats, a close audience in rural space.
This dark country lives like a rich, old cuss;
He found obscurity and it is us.

Palouse Farm Sonnet

III.

The summer I followed the smell of budding grain
to work and turned the farmer's rails muddy
brown with paint, splashed them thick until greased
with color—it dried but kept the gloss of rain.
And I would walk the farmer's hills and stain
the bugs with poison from a jug I carried
on my back until it bounced empty.
And other crops might catch the dust from planes.
In this place senses swim then drown;
stunned by just the water in a cup
or by a sky darkened and deep with zeal.
At dawn I sped a motorcycle down
the blank highway and held the camera up
trying to snap the joy in those green hills.

Night Skying

They tell the child
she might catch
cold running with the night sky
in her mouth like that.
Out in the post-dusk thrill
she plays—no companion
of a coat with its caution.
The scene is living on
the risk of leaves in piles,
brisk winds built by swinging
from a tree.
The chilled air dives
into her lungs,
a cage that breath can exit.

Now, the heart is smiling,
sifting through liquid
beating out life.
What good the taste
of dark oxygen,
steeped with starlight,
would do for them,
steaming the pane.

Epithalamion

We are twisted, bright
wicks rising up through wax.
Let fire melt
these clothes until we stand
fastened by light
blackened after spark
descends our fuse
and joins us in the heat
that shapes one name
through the dark,
the cold, the night
the end.

Angel Tiger

Christina Koning

Angel Tiger

She does have one memory of her father before his incarceration; although, given that she was but two years old at the time, it is as much about the cat. A kitten, he was still, all paws and eyes. Her father had picked him out of his coat pocket and dropped him into Polly's lap, little bristling orange thing that he was, with his tail sticking up and his pointed ears, that seemed too large for his face.

Her sister had cried out – as much in pleasure as alarm.

'Nay, do not scream so, for you will frighten him,' their father said, 'and then he may bite…'

This resulted in another access of screams and wriggling.

'Take him away, the nasty thing!' cried Polly, now really afraid, where she had been play-acting before.

'Do not call him so,' replied their father, scooping the little creature up out of harm's way. 'For he is of the tribe of Tiger, and therefore deserving of our respect… Are you not, Sirrah?' he went on, addressing the animal himself, which now lay quiet in the crook of his master's arm, its eyes that had flashed out green fire, narrowed to contented slits. A strange, soft roaring came from the tiger's throat.

'There, you see – he agrees with me,' said their father, sleeking the ruffled fur on the kitten's back with an index finger. 'He is not fierce, unless he is made angry, or afraid. Come, Bess, would you like to hold him? For he is at rest now, as you see…'

Then she had held out her arms, and her father had placed the sleeping cat into them. She had hardly dared to breathe, so anxious was she not to disturb him. The roaring sound grew louder, however, until it was as if she felt it within her own breast: a comforting music, like the soft ticking of a clock.

'You must hold him – so,' their father continued, the hand that had stroked the little cat's fur now smoothing down his elder daughter's tousled curls. 'Never upside-down – for he is not one of your dolls – and never by the tail. Nor must you serve him as I have seen you serve your sister, on occasion, with pinches and scolding. For he will not be scolded — being, as I have said, a respectable and dignified creature…'

These remarks he accompanied with kisses, which took away the least suggestion of severity. For he loved Polly above all others – even more than he loved their mother, and that was a great deal.

'Moreover,' their father was saying, still apropos of the cat, but perhaps having heard his wife's footsteps upon the stair, 'you must love him as you would a brother – for are you and he not of the same complexion?'

With this, he gave a tug to one of Polly's golden curls, so that she shrieked again, to their mother's consternation (she having just entered the room).

'Ah, here is another of the Tiger's tribe,' said their father, still in his waggish humour. And it was true that the colour of their mother's hair – a darker shade than Polly's – could not have been told apart from that of the cat.

At which observation, their mother only frowned.

'What nonsense are you filling their heads with now?' was all she said.

And whether Tigress or no, she was not best pleased by the newest addition to the household.

'For who is to feed it, and clean up its messes, if not I?' she complained. 'As if we did not have enough mouths to feed, you must bring us another…'

'Charity, dear wife, is a Christian virtue,' had been the reply. 'Unless they do not teach it in that Church of yours…'

After that, there was no more playing and no more laughter.

Instead of tumbling about on the floor with babies, her husband ought to be giving some thought to how they were to pay the rent, their mother said. Three months was owing, and Mr Newbery would not wait any longer. Nor was it right and fair that he *should* be made to wait…

'Even though he is your father.'

'He is not my father. He is my mother's husband.'

'Even so…'

'It makes no difference. We must still eat.'

'Ah, yes. And *drink*, too, you were going to say…'

'I did not say it.'

'No, but you *thought* it. I saw it in your eye.'

That was the beginning of a bad time.

She remembers but little of it, she is glad to say. Only that her father had been ill with fever, and had lain in bed for many days. She and Polly had been sent to stay with Mrs Fleming, across the way. She was fat, and cross, but sometimes she gave them sugar-plums.

When her father was recovered from his fever, he had begun praying. At first it was not very much – only at meal times, and when he went to bed; later, it got to be more often; nor did he leave off praying before his voice was hoarse. He would pray aloud in the street, and at all hours of the day. Once, in St James's Park, he prayed so loudly and so long that he routed all the company. The watchman had taken him up, and brought him home.

Soon it got so that he would knock on doors in the middle of the night, and demand that his friends should come down from their beds, and pray.

'For I bless the Prince of Peace and pray that all guns may be nailed up, save such as are for the rejoicing days,' he would cry. 'Rejoice in God, O ye tongues, give the glory to the Lord, and the Lamb...'

At last, it got so bad that Mr Newbery had locked him in his bedchamber, and taken away the key. He had shouted and wept for an hour, begging their mother to release him.

'Alas, alas! Have pity on me – a poor prisoner,' he cried. 'For I am in jeopardy, and they that should comfort me have turned their faces away...'

Their mother had told them to pay no attention, for their father was sick, she said. If he would learn to be quiet, he might grow better. But he had not grown better, and at last, he had been taken away. This was to Dr Battie's, in Shoreditch, where he was to be made well again. He had stayed there a year, during which they had not been permitted to visit. For the sight of those he had once loved might unsettle his mind, Mr Newbery said. Only when his wits had returned, would he be allowed to come home.

During that time, she had learned to read, and to write her name: Elizabeth Anne. She had told her father so the day he came back to Canonbury.

'Dear little Bess,' was his reply, 'you must give over reading, and writing, too – for it will only bring trouble upon you, as it has upon me.'

He had said little else, only reaching to stroke Polly's hair, in his old way.

For the rest of the time, it had seemed as if his mind were elsewhere. He had sat in his chair and gazed out of the window, at the trees that were swaying about in the wind. From time to time he had sighed, as if his heart would break.

There was no more rolling about the floor, and no more playing with the cat.

'For he, too, knows what it is to be a prisoner, having been my companion in adversity.'

To their mother and grandfather he had spoken not a word.

'They conspire against me,' he said. 'For I preach the very gospel of Christ, and yet they would have me shut up.'

And indeed it was not long before he was again taken away. A carriage had come, and waited in the street outside. There had been raised voices, the slamming of doors; then silence. She and Polly had been sent to bed, but they had sat on the landing and waited, until they heard the carriage drive away.

'We will never see Papa more,' Polly had said, and burst into a passion of tears.

She would rather not think about that time now. *Now* she must compose herself, and smile, and remember only that he is her father, to whom she owes (if nothing else) a duty of respect.

She folds her hands in her lap. Her gloves are new, and she has taken pains with her appearance. She is wearing her blue dress, and a new ribbon in her cap, and she has her best kid slippers on.

Polly said she might have spared herself the trouble.

'For where you are going will not be very pleasant or clean.'

'Will you not come with me?'

'You know that I cannot.'

In the end, her sister had relented enough to say that she would go with her to the door.

'But no further. I will wait for you in the carriage.'

She had had to content herself with that.

Now, as she sits waiting for the summons that will surely come soon (for Mr Smart had need of a few moments to tidy himself, said the bluff gentleman who had admitted her), she recalls the last time they met – her father and Polly, that is. Was it really nine years ago? It had been at the madhouse in Bethnal Green. She had also been there, but it was Polly who had had the worst of it. Their father had made her kneel down beside him on the floor of his cell, and had prayed aloud that she might be delivered from the power of the Adversary. That was his name for the Evil One.

Then he had wept, and said it was not her fault she was baptised a Moabite (his name for Catholics). No indeed, he had continued, for it was the fault of her mother...

At which Polly – then nine years old – had sprung up, and cried that he must not say bad things about Mama.

'Marianne, my dear child,' he had then said, quite gravely, 'do not weep so. For I would cut out my tongue before I would slander thy mother. It is only,' he went on, still kneeling before them (and how piteous was the expression in his eyes!) 'that I cannot bear the thought that either you or she should be in peril of your Immortal Souls, all for a fault which was of neither's choosing...'

At these last words, Polly had said she would stay to listen to no more.

'Come, Bess. Mama will be waiting.'

He had followed them to the door – where Dr Potter, having heard the disturbance, now stood to prevent his going further.

'It is not Bess I mean,' he had earnestly said. 'For she is baptised in the True Faith of Christ the Redeemer.'

'Goodbye, Father.'

'Fatherless children and widows are never deserted of the Lord...' came his voice, down the corridor, after them.

'I would to God our mother *were* a widow,' said Polly.

'You do not mean that,' she replied.

'Do not tell me what I mean, or do not mean! He believes me damned, and our mother too, all because we are baptised Catholics. You, of course, can count yourself safe...'

'Polly!'

'Do not speak to me, and - if you must speak - do not mention his name again.'

Nervously tapping her foot, in its fine kid slipper, on the dusty prison floor, she wonders if her father will talk to her of Redemption again. She very much hopes not. For while it is true that she, unlike her sister, was not baptised a Catholic – an agreement her parents had reached before she was born – she has spent the past three years being educated by the nuns at the Ursuline convent in Boulogne.

She is not sure if her father is aware of this fact, which seems calculated to annoy him. But then, she supposes that there is a great deal he does not know about her life. Not that she knows a great deal about his.

She knows he is a poet, because Mr Newbery told her:

'Your father had a fine intellect, before his troubles came on.'

He had won ever so many prizes for his verse, which had been much admired, her grandfather said. Dr Johnson and Mr Garrick had admired it, and Dr Burney, too – and they were none of them fools. It was a pity he had written nothing of any value since. In the madhouse, he had covered ream upon ream of paper, but it was all of it found to be trash…

Now, apparently cured of his madness, he is in prison once more. But since this – as he remarked in the letter she received from him a week ago – is for 'refusing to render unto Caesar that which is rightfully his', rather than for intemperate praying, she hopes that there will be no more talk of her immortal soul.

'Come, Miss.'

She follows the man upstairs, to her father's apartment. Even though it is a prison, it is not too bad, she sees. There is a sitting-room, in which her father sits, with a good (if threadbare) carpet upon the floor and some almost-decent furniture: two armchairs - a little broken-down; a table; four dining chairs. A bedchamber lies beyond. There are books, and papers. He has the freedom of the 'grounds', such as they are. Her uncle has purchased this small concession for him.

'How do you do, Father?'

The first shock is how thin and ill he has become – his complexion a bad yellow, his once-dark hair gone grey. He is dirty, too, her once-fastidious father, whose fondness for fine linen and silk waistcoats had nearly landed them in the poorhouse – 'if it had not been that he was sent to the madhouse first,' their mother had said, in a moment of bitterness.

Now his waistcoat is greasy with spilt food, and his coat-cuffs worn. His shirt is none-too-clean, and his neck-cloth a mere rag. Lowering her eyes from the contemplation of these distressing sights, she sees that there are holes in his shoes, and in his stockings, too…

'Well, Bess. I am glad to see you.'

At the sound of his voice, she lifts her gaze once more, and encounters his dark eyes. These, at least, are the same as she remembers them – although the sadness in them is enough to pierce her heart.

'No Polly with you, then?'

She shakes her head.

'Cat got your tongue?'

He is smiling as he says it, and she thinks, with relief, he is not mad.

'Where *is* the cat?' she thinks to ask.

Now it is her father's turn to shake his head.

'I have left him with Dr Burney. For I could not ask him – noble creature that he is – to share a prison cell. A madhouse, yes...'

'I remember he was with you at Bethnal Green,' she says.

'In the days of my jeopardy. Yes, yes...' He seems agitated at the remembrance. His words begin falling over themselves, in the old way. 'A terrible time,' he murmurs. 'A terrible time. We will not speak of it. No, no. We will not speak of it.'

He is silent a moment.

'At least here...' He spreads his arms wide to embrace the threadbare-carpeted room. 'There are no madmen – only publicans and sinners, and those, like myself, who have taken a vow of Poverty...'

'I am sorry to see you in such a sad case, Father.'

'Dear Bess. You were always kind-hearted. My kind-hearted child.' He regards her fondly, and for a moment, she basks in the warm glow of his attention. 'How old are you now? You must be sixteen at least...'

'I am seventeen, Father.'

He smiles.

'Quite the young lady. And what of your sister, Miss Marianne?'

'She is not well, else she would have come, too.'

The lie brings a blush to her cheek.

'That is a pity.'

Again, he falls silent.

'Mother is quite well,' she ventures.

But he says nothing to this. From outside, comes the sound of voices raised in anger.

'It is dinnertime,' he says, by way of explanation. Then seeing that she does not understand: 'They have given sixpence to the turn-key, to buy a piece of mutton, and he has returned with tuppence-worth. All the quarrels here are about money – as indeed is very often the case in the world outside...'

At this reminder of why she has come, she fumbles in her reticule. There is four guineas in her purse, and another two promised by Mr Carnan.

'Although it is better that your father does not have too much money about him,' her uncle had said. 'Given his unfortunate weakness – and the evil influences which surround that place…'

She places the purse upon the table.

If her father has given into his weakness lately, there is no sign of it – other than his bad colour; that, and the faint trembling of the hand he now stretches out to retrieve his prize.

'Thank you, my dear,' he says. 'I might have known that *you*, at least, would not desert me.'

She bows her head. Then for a while longer, they sit there without speaking.

On the windowsill is a pot of geraniums. He sees her looking at it.

'Red was ever my favourite colour. For it is a gift from God to gladden the sense of sight…'

At the mention of the Creator, she stiffens slightly. Perhaps, after all, he has not mended his ways…

But then he gives a rueful smile.

'I have not, of late, been on such intimate terms with God as I was wont to be.'

'No, Father.'

'You are a good girl, Bess. I wonder if you will understand me when I say that, though being mad was terrible, it is still more terrible not being mad…'

'I think I understand,' she says, although of course she does not.

He closes his eyes a moment.

'For in my nature I quested for beauty, but God, God hath sent me to sea for pearls,' he murmurs, so softly that she is not sure whether it is meant for her or no.

It does not seem the kind of remark that expects an answer, and so she says nothing.

'I had my vision,' he goes on. 'And very beautiful it was, with all its angels and demons; its lions and tigers and great Leviathans. Very terrible, too. Now it is gone – and with it, all my poetry…'

'You still have your poetry, Father.'

He opens his eyes.

'There, dear child, you are mistaken,' he says.

After this, he falls into a reverie, from which even the fact of her getting up to go barely rouses him. His eyes, once so bright, are cloudy now, and have an inward-looking gaze. As she bends to kiss him, she thinks how old and worn he has become, although he is not yet fifty. She straightens up, and he catches her by the wrist, detaining her a moment longer.

'Be sure and give my love to Polly,' he tells her.

'I will.'

She picks up her bag – now lightened of its burden – and moves towards the door, glancing back to where he sits, carelessly sprawled in the broken-backed chair. His gaze is directed, not towards her, but at something outside the window.

He does not seem to hear when she says goodbye.

Had she known, then, that it was the last time? She supposes that, in her heart, she must have known it.

She descends the stairs, to where the bluff man stands, paring his nails. He lets her out, and she walks across the prison yard. The turn-key opens the gate, and she crosses the street, to where the carriage is waiting.

As she does so, she looks up at the window that she knows to be his, and sees him standing there. She raises her hand, but if he sees her at all, he does not return her wave.

'You were a long time,' says Polly, as she gets into the carriage. 'I had almost given you up. What did he say to you? Was he very mad?'

'Oh no,' she says. 'Not mad at all. He sends his love.'

Her sister pulls a face. 'I do not want it.'

'You are hard to him,' she cannot forbear from saying.

Polly turns to look at her. 'And you have always been too soft,' she says. 'You seem to forget he broke our mother's heart.'

'I do not forget it,' she says.

As the carriage starts to move off, scattering the crowd of dirty children that has been hanging about it in the expectation of ha'pennies, she glances up at the place where her father was, hoping to catch sight of him again.

But the face at the window has gone, and the curtain is pulled across, so that it is as if no one was ever there at all.

Poems
David Shook

Silvestre Adán

As farmer

I've thumbed a thousand seeds into their
nests, I've asked them to grow tall as men.
Come chili. Come corn, come watercress.
Come plum and mango from your trees.
My knees are rough as cinder. My fingers
know the life of worms. I am a fish gone slack in
the net, tired of the river's silty tricks. Come sleep.

As artist

A dozen works by bare-bulb
each night till I lost my eyes,
one at a time. Rolled eighty
paintings each week & mailed
them to the beach. Went myself
to paint memories on shirts &
hats. My cousin still whines, derides
the shots & tits of cheap tourist shit.
Tits belong to cows, I tell him, Talk milk
or talk nice. Women liked my rabbits,
mid-leap. Men scorpions, teeth.

As orchard keeper

I feed the throat hum
of my suckpump with
a half-can of
lead free each day till
melons swell with promise and
you can smell the river on
the husks of corn two heads
taller than a man.

Evenings I feed the dogs,
sharpen my machete,
then hang in my hammock,
listen for rabbits & kids.
Mornings I swim across the
Balsas, wet my hair & pray for
rain, praise for watermelon.

As morning singer

Come chili. Come corn, come watercress.
Come plum and mango from your trees.

At the Baptist Seminary Dormitories in Mexico State

Earwigs drown in shared sinks, whirlpool down the drains
of cement showers splotched with paint from teams of

teens & chaperones descended from their heaven to roll more
coats on walls inches thick with sloppy layers of lead free.

Silverfish mate beneath the seminary pillows like sequins fucking.
One boy waits through the tuning half-snores, sighs, &

rolling readjustments of his roommates until their chorus joins the crickets,
night trucks, the hall's fluorescent buzz. Soundtrack to

his dull & guilty masturbation. Week's end he'll leave his shoes &
most shirts to practice sacrifice,

save one, bunched between his wool poncho & Dopp kit,
strings of dead semen starched like sweat.

A wasp hive hangs from the chapel awning, papered tombs'
doors rolled back to reveal their peanut shell interiors, empty.

I Know Your Body

after Víctor Terán

If you were a city
I could give perfect directions
to wherever they asked me,
I could map your neighborhoods &
catalogue your smells.

If you were a city
I would get lost every day
down some new corridor.
I would toss my map, hitchhike through
your suburbs, wander your downtown.

Our Obsidian Tongues

A translation from the Classical Nahuatl of Tecuani

Our tongues are neither spoons
nor arrows. Neither flower petals
nor leaves. Our tongues are
obsidian tongues, shorter than
the knives priests use to sacrifice
but equally sharp. Our tongues
flint sparks. Our tongues chip
thin flakes when stabs
aren't straight & quick. Our
tongues are neither spoons
nor arrows, petals nor leaves.
Our obsidian tongues.

By Way of Introduction

A translation from the Spanish of Moisés Náufrago

There are more honest men in the government than in my family.
My brothers make promises they cannot keep but they cannot afford

to print free tee-shirts, they are too lazy to be rich.

I have fasted for three weeks, eating only the maguey worms
curled around the edges of the bottles I empty, swollen like

nipples with milk. There's more blood in the hymnbook than my liver.

I gave confession to my priest but he fell asleep—
I know god stays awake laughing at my sins, but

I can't tell if he laughs because of happiness or pity.

For one month I have only spoken in octosyllable & rhyme, save for
my poems & insults. Drunk women love my cadence until I've stripped

them in the sack—one thrust per seven syllables is simply not enough.

My mother couldn't decide to name me Shitface or Nothing,
so my father made the choice. I am his favorite joke, the pharaoh's

son, the mumble-tongue, the lost for forty years.

Listen, Christ, I am Saint Thomas on his knees. Let me lick your holy hip,
bite its scab & taste its blood like a rusted nail beneath my tongue,

decide if you are real.

Praise Song for Santiago Matamoros

A translation from the Spanish of Moisés Náufrago

I praise you for knowing us from Moors,
for recognizing our skin not as their desert leather,
our hearts not as their small stones, like the pits of
dates or apricots.

I praise you for your wooden ears.
They do not ring through our hourly barrage of
rockets, buzz of sparklers beneath your
concrete dome.

I praise you for mezcal, tequila, beer,
unnamed liquors in their faded plastic two-liters.

I praise you for revenge, for mosquitos' fine palate for
imported blood, for dengue, malaria, E. coli, some cholera.

For guilt.

I praise you for the dam they couldn't build.

For the cattle-killer scorpions whose black tails
lick the ankles of thieves, know their prey by
scent & heart alone.

I praise you for mezcal, again.

I praise you, Santiago Matamoros,
Santiago Mataindios, Black Santiago on
your cloudy horse.

David Shook

Questions to Help Identify a Pale Tongue

Does his tongue crinkle like paper money?[1]

Does his breath smell like copper & sweat?
Like the palm of a hand in a pocket with change?[2]

Can he roll his Rs? Can he roll them without pause?[3]

Are his eyes the color of the dollar bill, the color
of the sky? Coffee with more milk than yours?[4]

---

1   My tongue flaps like a dollar bill.
2   Like a coin beneath the tongue. My teeth are plaqued with nickel.
3   Yes. Mostly.
4   The green of currency faded in the wash.

LAZY*eye*

Nicholas McInerny

Synopsis

Prentice and Murmygan, both late forties, were at Oxford University together twenty five years ago. Now both highly successful, they bump into each other in the Oyster bar at Convent Garden during a performance of Rigoletto. Murmygan, an eye surgeon, notices Prentice has something wrong with his left eye. He offers to examine it....

Scene 2.

Both men have their jackets off and bowties untied, collars loose.

PRENTICE is seated, leaning forward, having his right eye examined. MURMYGAN on a seat opposite, holding a piece of equipment in his hand, with levers and handles and buttons. Elaborate but he manipulates it expertly.

MURMYGAN
They start arriving before dawn, gathering at the edge of the forest.

PRENTICE
How do you know?

MURMYGAN
The fires in the trees. They come from villages for miles around – often walking for days, up to a week even.

PRENTICE
Who?

MURMYGAN
The women mainly. The woman are always braver. Defying their husbands or mothers-in-law. Sometimes even smuggling their children out of the village against the wishes of the village elders.

PRENTICE
Some voodoo shit?

MURMYGAN
Witchipoo and whale music, third world style. Ignorance and superstition and good old fashioned nastiness wrapped up in some… some….

PRENTICE
It's alright, you can say it.

MURMYGAN
Some toothless blackened old stick of a crone dressed in bangles and Nike trainers!

They both relax at the transgression. MURMYGAN steps back to adjust the equipment.

To defy that is like shaking your fist at God but they do, they defy. When they hear about the plane arriving they pick up their kids and come. Twenty miles, thirty. Walking out of dust and ignorance to the hospital with wings.

MURMYGAN goes over to fetch another piece of equipment. He starts connecting the two pieces. He works quickly and effortlessly.

That year was spectacular. We got to try new techniques, pioneering stuff, we worked like slaves, long *long* days in Theatre. The patients became a blur, one after the other. Just shapes and names. Statistics.

But it was exciting. Raising the veil, giving back sight to so many. It was work without limits!

MURMYGAN moves back over.

So I didn't really notice the lad who turned up on the last afternoon. Moon faced? Pot bellied? Spindle legged? Possibly. Aged ten I'd guess but how could you tell? They were all ancient.

Nor his mother either. Squatting patiently in her shawl whilst I examined him. The heat was nuclear.

However, I do remember him when he died, about an hour later, on the operating table.

> **PRENTICE**
> He died?

> **MURMYGAN**
> Complications. Internal haemorrhage.

MURMYGAN sits and leans forward with the equipment.

> Look up.

> There is always a risk with a weak heart.

> And down.

> I hate losing a patient. It puts me in a foul mood.

> **PRENTICE**
> You don't blame yourself.

> **MURMYGAN**
> Of course I don't. Why would I do that?
> I was doing the best job under the circumstances.

> **PRENTICE**
> More than.

> **MURMYGAN**
> Exactly.
> Blame is redundant.
> Blame isn't part of the equation.

> Up again.

MURMYGAN makes an adjustment to the equipment.

We gave the boy's body back to his mother. She said nothing. Just nodded once or twice and this completely unfathomable smile.

MURMYGAN pauses a moment, back in the moment

Later that night we heard the women wailing around the fires, saw their shadows in the trees. In the morning they were gone.

He forces himself to focus...

> Now the left eye please.

> The following year we went back.

> Right.

Now MURMYGAN sees something in the corner of PRENTICE's
left eye.
> ...And hold it.
> Just there, yes.
> *Hold!*

*He leans forward. The two men very close now – staring at
each other through the eye piece.*

Silence.

*It builds between them. Active and passive. A gathering
intensity.*

PRENTICE
What is it? What can you see?

*MURMYGAN moves away quickly, wanting to put distance between
them. He dismantles the equipment with casual roughness,
almost violently.*

You can see something, can't you.

MURMYGAN
Like I said, the following year we went back. We went back
and I don't know what I was expecting. But somehow when I
saw her I wasn't surprised.

PRENTICE
The mother?

MURMYGAN
She'd been waiting for me. She came charging over the runway
and up the stairs to the plane, eyes glaring, shouting, *in
pieces!* Me standing there and this tiny woman waving her
hands!

PRENTICE
Jesus…

MURMYGAN
That's what I thought. This is it, I braced myself. I mean
how do you argue with grief?

PRENTICE
You can't. It's the best excuse for the worst behaviour.

MURMYGAN throws down the equipment hard, carelessly. It
clatters.

MURMYGAN
And then the translator stepped up
The translator said and I remember this exactly:
'She wants to tell you this.
The Well did not dry up once last year.
Parts for the Purifier came quickly
All the crops grew.
My children are fat and
the goats give more milk
and my husband is happy and sings all day.
Only three people died from the Catching Cough
but they were as old as the stones.
Now we have two generators and
a solar powered mobile.
We sometimes watch your *Strictly Come Dancing* from
England.

The village has been blessed since I made
the sacrifice of my son.
Since his death our lives are so blessed'

There's a silence.

PRENTICE
A sacrifice?

MURMYGAN
That's right.

PRENTICE
What? She thought you… you deliberately…

> **MURMYGAN**
> Deliberate or not.

PRENTICE
Sacrificed her son?

> **MURMYGAN**
> Yes

PRENTICE
A *sacrifice?*

> **MURMYGAN**
> Part of the *deal.*

PRENTICE
(*what?*)…

> **MURMYGAN**
> That meant good things could happen.
> Their lives improved.

PRENTICE
Because her son died?

> **MURMYGAN**
> Her village flourished.
> Her life grew better.
> Her husband sings.

PRENTICE
And brings her roses every day. Shit, you don't believe
that.

> **MURMYGAN**
> She did.
> Everyone in her village did.
> His death for the greater good.
> His death *necessary.*

PRENTICE
But you don't fucking actually believe that!

MURMYGAN goes over to his jacket, fishes in the pocket.

MURMYGAN
Does it matter what I think?
I didn't walk for days to thank someone.
This woman walked for days!
She knelt at my feet and kissed my hand and in a flash turned
everything I'd ever learnt about medicine into *dust!*

MURMYGAN hands PRENTICE a small object – polished and hard
and shiny from being constantly handled. Impenetrable.

She even bought me this.

PRENTICE
A piece of fossilised goat shit?

MURMYGAN
It's bone actually.
It's considered very precious.
Some kind of… of relic.

PRENTICE holds it up and examines it.

PRENTICE
So you felt honoured.

MURMYGAN
It mattered to them.

PRENTICE
One woman's offering to the great high priest.

MURMYGAN
Carl…

PRENTICE
Some ethnic twattery…

MURMYGAN
Alright.

PRENTICE
You let it make a *difference.*

MURMYGAN

I was sideswiped. It caught me unawares.

MURMGYAN

And now you have to take it everywhere?

MURMYGAN

Yes, well…

PRENTICE

Jesus you do…

MURMYGAN

I know it's ridiculous…

PRENTICE

Fuck, no. We all need a little voodoo in our lives.
Even when we go to the Opera.
Even in the Oyster bar at Covent Garden,
humming Rigoletto.

MURMYGAN

I don't expect you to understand.
I hardly understand it myself.

PRENTICE turns and lobs it carelessly right across the room to MURMYGAN who catches it, just.

PRENTICE laughs out loud, forced conviviality.

PRENCTICE

Still useful in the slips then.

MURMYGAN doesn't answer.

Still play? Still enjoy the slap of willow on ball?

MURMYGAN

When I can.

PRENTICE

I bet you turn out, regular as clockwork. Every Sunday, the papers read, the Shares checked, the wife serviced – and it's on with the whites, the bag slung in the boot, a quick

drive to the Heath, some light classical. Verdi? Schubert
Lieder?

One Oxford habit you acquired for a lifetime, huh?

*PRENCTICE laughs again, but softer, darker. His face
resolves.*

Christ.
So much for the droit de seigneur, my friend.
So much for the divine right of kings.

MURMYGAN crosses back to his jacket.

MURMYGAN
I shouldn't have told you.
You haven't changed.

PRENTICE
What did you expect? Sympathy?

PRENTICE
Something

PRENTICE
A sentimental moment?
A brotherly arm around the shoulder?
I can do better than that.

MURMYGAN
Listen, not even my wife knows.

PRENTICE
Of course not, she wouldn't understand.
Wonderful woman, I'm sure, but she doesn't have the first
fucking clue.

MURMYGAN
I love my wife, Carl.

PRENTICE
We all love our wives.
Why do you think we keep secrets from them?

MURMYGAN
(Understand?)

PRENTICE goes to MURMYGAN, grabs his arm.

PRENTICE
How could she? How could she?
She wasn't there right at the beginning,
like I was.
She wasn't there at the Porters Lodge on that grey October
afternoon,
when you appeared, heart in mouth,
dragging a suitcase, full of grammar school pride
and provincial lust and drunk-fucked by the
history of it, by the sheen of prestige,
stuck out your hand which was trembling.
Trembling!
Am I right?
Am I right?

MURMYGAN is transfixed now.

All that ambition.
All that appetite.
All that unbridled and volcanic talent,
We hardly knew about, you and I,
Waiting inside us,
under our crucifying shyness,
Waiting to be unleashed on the world,
to take its rightful place,
achieve its potential,
to seek its full expression!

PRENTICE swells.

And you know what I believe?
Between friends,
Candidly,
Between old friends twenty five years on,
hasn't it worked out well?
Hasn't it worked out bloody marvellously well
for the both of us?
And you want to know why?

PRENTICE leans in.

Because I believe although talent makes its own argument in
the world,
great talent makes argument impossible!
And with genius the world bows down!

*PRENTICE brings his hands together hard, lets the word
hang.*

MURMGYAN
Genius?

PRENTICE
You idiot. Thank God I'm here.

MURMYGAN
Genius?

PRENTICE
You saw immediately, in my left eye.
The moment after we shook hands and got over
our surprise – 'God it's you! It's *really* you!'
The moment I ordered a drink and in my excitement
spilt it.
You said, forgive me for asking, Carl, but this is my area.
Are you having problems with your peripheral vision?
Are you misjudging depth of field?

*There was something wrong with my eye
...And you knew.*

MURMYGAN
Alright. I knew.

PRENTICE
Respect is due. All hail to the king.

MURMYGAN
Piss off.

PRENTICE
Now tell me what's wrong.

MURMYGAN
You need an operation.

PRENTICE
Operation?

MURMYGAN
There's a flaw.

PRENTICE
A flaw?

MURMYGAN
A tiny flaw. Left untreated it could become something serious.

PRENTICE
How serious?

MURMYGAN
You'll want a second opinion.

PRENTICE
Fuck.

MURMYGAN
So the sooner it's operated on…

PRENTICE
How soon?

MURMYGAN
Don't dawdle.

PRENTICE stares down. He makes a decision.

Don't worry. They'll love you. It'll be written up in all the journals.

PRENTICE
A tiny teeny *fascinating* flaw.

MURMYGAN
It won't take long. It's a very specific intervention.

PRENTICE
Specific?

MURMYGAN
Local anaesthetic.

PRENTICE
Awake?

MURMYGAN
But this is the thing. You'll need to be absolutely still.

PRENTICE
What? As in….

MURMYGAN
A statue, yes. Immobile. *Motionless.* There must be no movement at all.

PRENTICE
Submit to the knife. Be at your mercy.

MURMYGAN
If you like. Yes. Because the cut is so delicate, so subtle, ten thousandths of a millimetre, smaller - one slip and…

It's like dancing on the head of a …

A half understanding:

Submit…

MURMYGAN breaks off. PRENTICE is staring at him. Now he realises.

MURMYGAN is appalled, but he's excited too. Really thrilled.

No. Oh no.

             PRENTICE
             Why not?

             MURMYGAN
        You're not actually suggesting….

             PRENTICE
             Why not?

MURMYGAN
Here? Now?

PRENTICE
Is it possible?

MURMYGAN
Are you mad?

PRENTICE
I trust you.
You're my oldest friend.
My faith in you is boundless.

MURMYGAN
(Jesus Christ on a bicycle!)

PRENTICE
That's not an answer.

MURMYGAN
Okay, how about it's midnight, I've had three glasses of champagne,
you've got a driver in a car outside,
and this…this….all this….*fucking hell, Carl!*

MURMYGAN is suddenly still

How about a million other things?

Sacred Properties

Sarah Darby

Sacred Properties

A balled up piece of paper landed on Tom's stomach. He sat up, shook his head, and started to smooth the page out. It was page one of *So you're going to have a heart valve replacement?* Harry held the next page ready to tear like a threat.

Tom ignored him, and began to twist and fold the page until it was a graceful paper plane. He aimed and it sailed over Harry's head, curling in a circle and landing in the corner of the room.

'Beat that.'

Harry retrieved the paper and unfolded it, one crease at a time, to see how it was made. He tore the next page out and swiftly formed a duplicate plane.

'Too easy.'

The corridor was the obvious place to have the contest. The vinyl floor had convenient marker lines to measure distance.

'We'll throw together.' Tom straightened his pyjama top and blew out two or three hard breaths. Harry jogged from foot to foot like a boxer.

'Come on then.'

'On three. One, two – '

Their arms clashed, Harry slammed into the wall, bounced back into Tom and knocked him down and his drip stand too. They lay swearing and rubbing their bony knees and elbows.

'Finely tuned athletes, the pair of you.' Bridget helped Tom up and straightened the heavy metal stand, but Harry scrambled up unaided.

'I'm fine.'

A trickle of blood ran down his elbow. The flow grew thicker and dripped onto the floor. Bridget wrenched Harry's arm above his head and squeezed firmly. Her fingers grew slippery.

'How long since you had a warfarin test?'

Harry grunted.

'What?'

'The phlebotemist hasn't been in for ages,' said Tom. 'I don't think he likes us.'

'I don't want to know. Hop and press the call button then.'

Tom duly hopped, while Bridget held Harry and his pointing arm.

Two hours later, the pressure dressing around Harry's arm had turned his fingers more blue than usual, but the bleeding had stopped. His test for warfarin levels had come back.

'Congratulations. You're at the top of the leaderboard.' Bridget came in with the result and a plastic cup.

'How high is it?' Harry thought about his blood running thin.

'Well, I wouldn't advise shaving for a while. Drink this.' Bridget held the cup to Harry's lips before he could slowly bend his elbow to take it himself. He opened his mouth to protest and she threw the liquid down.

'Sorry, but it tastes awful and the best way is to get it over with.'

'Look on the bright side,' said Tom, when Harry was swilling lucozade round and round his mouth to try and get rid of the vitamin K taste.

'What bright side?' He didn't quite swallow before he spoke and a trace of orange fizz appeared on his lip.

'She thought you were man enough to shave.'

*

'They really work well, don't they?'

Tom decided he couldn't see the edges of the ceiling tiles and let a satisfied warmth run through him. The constant electric light had become their latest enemy. The covers they had made for the safety lights were their fifth prototypes and easily the most effective. They were made from the plastic cups from the water-dispenser, coloured in black with a marker pen. Afterwards, each of Harry's fingers was stained purple-black down to the first joint.

Tom had been on guard while Harry fitted a cup over each bulb holder. Harry had to push the cup on smoothly and firmly, without cracking the thin plastic. He had to stretch up and re-colour each cup where his damp fingertips rubbed off the ink. He had to do all this with his legs braced like a surfer, balanced on Tom's bed because it had the slightly firmer mattress.

They fitted one cup each afternoon during handover, when they were convinced no-one was watching their monitor displays. There were five bulbs to tackle and for four nights they had waited for someone on duty to notice the light dimming.

'Enjoy it while it lasts.' Harry listened to scuffling from Tom's bed.

'Are you doing something I don't want to be in the room for?'

'I'm going to look out of the window.'

Tom reached the glass and rested his forehead against it. For the first time in weeks, he couldn't see himself apart from a liquid flash reflecting his eyes. The radiator burned through his thin pyjamas to his shins, but he stayed where he was, taking in the sky.

'So what are we looking at?' said Harry.

'There's still too much pollution.'

'We're in a city. What do you expect?'

'Light pollution, I meant. All that glow from the other wards is getting in the way.'

'But electric's always going to be brighter than a star a million miles away, isn't it?'

'Are you kidding? Venus is bright enough to cast shadows on a clear night.'

'Venus is a star?'

Tom rubbed his palm over his forehead. 'I thought you said you read that Star Guide? Venus is a planet.'

'Alright, it's a planet, I get it.' Harry stomped back to bed and thumped his pillow.

Tom followed him. Even in the almost-dark, he could see Harry had his thick paperback shielding his face. It had a dragon and a dagger on the cover, both dripping blood.

'How's the book?'

'Too much talking, not enough sex.' Harry threw it on the floor and faced the wall.

'You talk a good game yourself but I've not seen a queue building up to give you a sponge bath. I reckon you're just reading bits out of your dodgy magazines.'

Tom heard Harry roll back to face him. He took this as a good sign.

'Oh come on, tell me, have you really done much?'

'Much what?'

'Much ... not talking.'

'Not since I got in here.'

'That was all talk about you and the pharmacist then?'

'She had such a great arse.' Harry sighed.

'But she thought you were an arse?'

'Some crap about being too young.'

'Did you tell her you had the heart of a fifty-year-old chain-smoker?'

They lapsed into ceiling-watch. There was the sound of something heavy being wheeled down the corridor. When it was quiet again, Harry said,

'So when are you going to get past talking with your "friend"?'

'Who?'

'The one with all the bracelets, always hanging around.'

'We're just friends.'

'For her maybe. I've seen puppies with more dignity than you.'

'I'm not interested in her like that.'

'Uh-huh. What colour are her eyes?'

'Hazel.'

'You're interested.'

'Because I know what colour her eyes are?'

'Because if you were just friends, you'd have said "brown".'

*

'Well, that's rubbish.' Tom pointed at the screen with his fork and a globule of gravy dripped onto the floor.

'I know. She'd never be able to do that with her hand if she really had a needle in it.'

Tom and Harry were watching '*Casualty*' on television. It marked the end of the week, as regularly as the shepherd's pie and washed-out french beans. They had a competition to spot the medical impossibilities.

'Look at that!' Harry waved at the screen. 'If he's had a stroke I'm Linford Christie.'

'Show us your six-pack then.'

Harry turned off Tom's television using his own remote control. It was a battle that often lasted all night. Both the televisions were the same model, with identical controls. They were so close together that one lazy point of the remote could change either machine. Mostly, laziness had nothing to do with it. They both wore headphones to hear different programmes. Tom's were enormous padded sound-engineer's that made him look as though he flew a second world war plane. Harry had tiny ear-pieces that didn't mess up his hair. He took great delight in waiting until Tom was watching the climax of a thriller, then changing his channel onto MTV. Tom reckoned Harry had given him a number of unofficial cardioversions that way.

Tom's tally of official versions of that procedure was already impressive. It was a neutral sounding term for what happened. Tom's heart was only sixteen years old, but it was tired. Like a weary horse galloping home, its stride would falter, the legs tangle together and the rhythm would be lost. The chambers of Tom's heart slipped into syncopation and couldn't find the beat.

He no longer even looked at the consent form he signed, blotting his name to acknowledge risk of stroke, risk of death, risk of brain damage. When he woke after the short anaesthetic, his heart would be quietly behaving underneath two scalded pink squares where the paddles had released a jolt through him. He imagined the marionette jerk and wondered whether anyone held his arms and legs down. There were never any marks on them.

*

A trickle of people in surgical scrubs had been visiting Harry all day. When Tom woke up after a sleep in the afternoon, another one had arrived and pulled the curtain around as if that cloaked their conversation. Tom heard Harry giving them a predictably hard time. He struggled upright in the bed and felt around on the floor for his slippers. By the time he had one foot secure, the curtain was yanked back and a man strode out.

'What did he want?'

'As if you didn't hear.'

'I just woke up for the insults about his mother.'

'Well, you heard the best bit then.'

'Do you want to do something tonight?'

'Are you asking me out?' Harry snorted.

'Yeah, I've been building up to it for weeks.'

'I'm dead slow at picking up on signs, me.'

'Is this the best place you could think of?' Harry swung the carrier bags from one hand and dragged himself up another set of stairs.

'It'll be worth it,' gasped Tom, who was almost a whole flight behind. He had his binoculars around his neck, but Harry had long since taken over carrying everything else.

Finally, there were no more stairs to climb. Only a grey fire escape door secured with a heavy chain. Harry watched Tom produce a key from his chest pocket and undo the padlock.

'How in hell did you get hold of that?'

Tom refused to answer. The door resisted them both until they turned around, braced their legs, and pushed hard with their backs on the count of three. It slammed open and they stumbled outside onto the roof.

'Fucking amazing.' Harry went straight to the edge and looked down. Tom stood in the doorway and stared up at the sky. He dragged his attention back and laid the security chain three or four times over the doorframe to block it open. Now he could relax and step away.

'Who on earth bought beer for you? You only look about twelve.' Harry took a can.

'Had it delivered. If you've got a credit card, you can order anything.'

'You don't have a credit card.'

'But that surgeon used to.'

'And you used to be such a nice boy.'

Tom passed the food to Harry without comment. He had ordered all the foods he had heard Harry fantasise about during meal-times. Harry was raking through a festival of saturated fat and salt. He obliged Tom by taking a brief look through the proffered binoculars from time to time, but mainly he chewed. When Tom placed the moulded plastic eye-pieces over his eyes, the rooftop disappeared and he was part of the night air. He could see shapes as familiar as friends' faces.

'Tomorrow.' Harry clunked his beer can against Tom's, making both cans foam down the sides.

Tom looked at Harry's outline. He licked his lips and felt he should say something wise.

'To tomorrow. You'll be fine.'

Light was creeping into the sky around them, showing their grey faces peeking out of the blankets draped around their shoulders.

'Will you do something for me?' Harry asked.

'Depends.'

'You're supposed to say yes. 'Depends' is just an insult.'

'Well, what is it?' Tom rubbed his eyes. Harry took the moment while Tom wasn't looking at him and spoke fast,

'Read those patient booklets to me.'

'Why?'

'Never mind.'

'OK, where are they?'

Harry pulled the thick stack of papers from his blanket. The pale sky offered just enough light to make out the small print. Tom started to read aloud.

*

Since their night on the roof, Harry's surgery date had been changed three times but the latest target was tomorrow. Tom found himself sneaking looks at Harry instead of facing him. There was a fascination in the place he was about to go, his decision to let hands reach into his chest.

They were used to each other's pale blue faces and fingernails, concave chests that had been repeatedly opened and closed since their hearts had first betrayed problems as babies. Symptoms came and symptoms went and it seemed to them there was only a sporadic connection to what lay beneath the smooth scalpel lines curved over their ribs.

After dinner, Tom couldn't pretend any more that the expression on Harry's face was anything other than fear. He didn't know what to say. He offered his binoculars, slung as always from the bedframe.

'Want to go and have a look for that pharmacist?'

Harry managed a partial smile. 'S'alright.'

'They say you'll be back in a couple of days.'

'That's what they say.'

Harry looked more tired than Tom had ever seen him. Some of his drugs had been stopped ready for the operation. They weren't supposed to cause any problems, but Tom had a churning in his stomach.

'I'll keep your bed warm for you,' he said.

'Oh yeah?'

'Yeah, it's a long walk to the bathroom in the night.'

'They invented waterproof mattresses for bastards like you.'

Tom flicked through the channels on his television. Harry lay still and mute and Tom had a flicker of what the room would be like while he was on his own. The sense that something would happen each day, that's what Harry brought along with his screwed up black t-shirts and rancid socks. Now Tom would have to go back to pretending to revise and trying to persuade the cleaner into a broken conversation to fill another five minutes. At least it wouldn't be for long. He should plan something really, he decided. Something to welcome Harry back again. He'd be a bit fragile probably, so no collapsing chairs or anything. He drummed his fingers on his thigh while he thought, feeling happier by imagining the few days by himself already over.

'Going to — ' Harry rushed out half a sentence and stopped.

He must have fallen asleep. It took a few seconds before Tom realised Harry hadn't had his arms in the air. He could never fall asleep without doing that first, never. Tom called out, something that wasn't a word, just a long loud noise that he kept making. Harry didn't respond. Bridget stuck her head round the door and Tom pointed, running out of breath. She stepped smartly over to Harry, pressed the button on the wall and said,

'Put on your mask, Tom. Breathe in.'

He heard her but couldn't move. He watched, his eyes stinging from not blinking. At the corner of what he could see was the still figure of Harry, no longer on his side but rolled flat onto his back and barricaded by uniforms.

Other staff arrived, and then more. Those others started to run, their feet slapping on the vinyl, hurrying in and out for trolleys and the black plastic suitcase that looked like it should have an electric drill in it. When they opened it, Tom saw a row of syringes and ampoules where there should have been drill bits.

Tom hugged his knees to the loose scar on his chest. They pulled the curtains round his bed with such force that half the material tore free from the hooks and flapped open. He glimpsed a stocky man straddling Harry, hands locked together and pressed to his chest as if he was pushing one breath at a time back into him. He was pushing too hard. Harry looked tiny underneath him. Tom thought he could hear his breastbone crack under the pressure. The image stained itself onto the inside of his eyelids and he could see nothing else. He pressed his fists into his eye sockets while they wheeled Harry's bed past, and felt the needles in the backs of his hands pulse with the strain.

Someone put their hand on his shoulder but he didn't move. Bridget gently stretched the elastic strap of the oxygen mask over his head, but it caught on his ears. He knew it was her from her smell, a kind of powdery scent that caught in his throat in a good way. She lifted one of his hands at a time to slip the mask down his face and he kept his eyes closed. He felt the flow of oxygen like water over his face and pretended he was a fish underwater, swimming free.

No-one came back. Tom told himself it was a good sign, that they were too busy saving Harry to need to come and give bad news. His finger hovered over the call button but he didn't want to pull anyone away from Harry. He tried to read, tried to listen to the scrolling news headlines repeated over and over on the radio through the night, tried to close his eyes. For the past three hours and forty minutes they had been resolutely open. He watched the sky turn from black to grey to coloured. He counted whatever he could think of to count, to measure the wait. When he ran out of things, he counted how many times he moved his foot on the scratchy sheet, as if his limb was unconnected to him and had to be monitored. He crouched on his bed like a life-raft, staying as small as he could. If he could just keep the world in balance, not rock too much, it would carry on like before.

The Country Where I Love You

Annette Pas

The Country Where I Love You

Part I: Bérénice

Chapter 1

Bérénice is my brother's daughter. When he died, in 2003, Bérénice was placed in an institution. I went to visit her there. Meneer Abdullah, my good friend and a greater expert on women and children than I shall ever be, came with me for moral support and practical guidance. He trimmed his beard. He dressed up in his only Western suit.

'No room for false pride today,' he offered as an explanation. 'Today is an important day, you may well end up becoming a father. It is best to make a good impression.'

By way of cultural compromise, he kept his little multicoloured hat, ornamented for the occasion with a green feather borrowed from his parrot. I was wearing my father's wedding suit, way over half a century old as we both were, and dabbing my forehead with one of my late mother's biggest handkerchiefs, kept for crisis situations.

'It's not at all certain she'll come to live with me,' I said while squeezing my long spindly legs into Meneer Abdullah's small dented pale blue van. I sat down on something hard, removed an old horseshoe from underneath me and threw it over my shoulder into the back before I added:

'They might think it best for her to stay in the institution.'

'How do you mean, best for her? She's your child now.' Meneer Abdullah raised his eyebrows. 'Who is they?'

'The government, people in the institution, people who are qualified to look after children.'

'But you are family!' said Meneer Abdullah, 'How much more qualified can you be? She's the child of your brother, isn't she?'

'Yes.'

'And there are no other relatives?'

'No.'

Bérénice's mother was a woman with purple curly hair who had lived with my brother for a while but left him soon after the child was born.

'Then she belongs to you now. Anyone who dares to claim otherwise isn't from a very good family background himself. Don't worry, I will help you explain it all to those government people,' Meneer Abdullah spoke with much vigour, clenching the steering wheel as if holding the reins of a high spirited steed. When we approached the ring road, he dug his spurs into the flanks, cut off two huge lorries on his way to the left lane and only jammed on the brakes once, when spotting a police car that was hiding in the bushes. The horseshoes in the back and I, too were flying backwards and forwards to the rhythm of Meneer Abdullah's impulsive driving. I was glad to have brought along three handkerchiefs. The first one was already soaked and we were not even halfway.

'I'm not sure whether it would really be best for her to come and live with me,' I said. 'I am sixty three years old and I've no experience of looking after anything but myself, which I find hard enough as it is.'

'You have a dog!' Meneer Abdullah contradicted me passionately.

'I'm not sure if the er... people of the government would find that a sufficient guarantee. After all I don't know the first thing about raising children.'

'Don't worry. You're human. It comes naturally,' was Meneer Abdullah's prompt reply.

The things that had come to me naturally hadn't all been that good.

'What if I'm the only person on earth to whom it doesn't come naturally?' I asked.

'Then I'll help you. Stop worrying, my friend! We'll all help you! What is she like anyway, this god-given child?'

'Er... rather small, last time I saw her.'

I had seen Bérénice once when she was a baby. After Bérénice's mother left him, my brother traded our homeland for the more progressive Netherlands and I visited him a few times in his rather chaotic house in Amsterdam. I remembered seeing Bérénice sitting in a corner, building little houses with bricks and using beer mats for a roof. She always wore these tiny pink pyjamas with two little grey elephants on her breast, their trunks forming a heart in the centre. In those days I usually stayed far away from women – and by extension, children – but I do remember talking to Bérénice once. The risk of doing something wrong to an already motherless child in my brother's already messy living room must have appeared rather small to me. When my brother went to the kitchen for a beer, I walked over to the corner where the child was sitting. I inspected her brick constructions.

'Your foundations are rather weak,' I told her and then I tried to show her how she could build her houses higher if she used more bricks in the first layer. She moved a little away from me but looked at the movements of my hands with much interest. How old would she have been then? Standing up she'd have had the height of an average keeshond (without the tail); not yet quite tall enough to start reaching door handles when balancing on its back legs.

Meneer Abdullah interrupted my thoughts.

'Ah, soon she will grow into a beautiful daughter who will make you proud. I know it!' he said with the same conviction he tells me every Christmas that soon my house too will be filled with the voices of women and children. Then he put his foot down to cut off a BMW on his way to the exit. The BMW flashed its lights and hooted.

'Ah, very friendly people on the road today,' said Meneer Abdullah. He waved enthusiastically. Before I realized what I was doing, I waved too. Then I needed both hands to grab onto my seat as Meneer Abdullah took the exit.

'Bé-ré-nice!' Meneer Abdullah exclaimed while changing gears. 'A name for a princess! Berenika, Berenike, Bérénice! A woman who will write history,' he concluded. 'She'll be grateful for having been able to return to the country of her ancestors at last, wouldn't you think?'

Indeed, Bérénice had spent the first years of her life in Amsterdam, where my brother had lived happily until he was tragically run over by a milk van. In his last words, he expressed discontent with the Dutch milk van driver and the specific wish that his daughter be brought up on Belgian soil. That's why Bérénice had been brought over to an institution in the province of Antwerp.

'Have you got a map with you?' I asked Meneer Abdullah. 'I've never been there before but I imagine they want us to be on time. We'd better not get lost.'

Meneer Abdullah pointed at the glove compartment. I found many maps but our insignificantly small land of beer and lost battles wasn't on any of them.

An hour later (and exactly one minute before the official ending of the visiting hour) Meneer Abdullah parked his steed on the parking lot of the institution. I'm afraid he parked it on a place which was reserved for the steeds of slightly higher up knights, but he couldn't be persuaded to move it.

'That sign means it's for important people or emergency situations. And we're both, because we've come to welcome a new child into your family!'

I was already getting through my second handkerchief, sweat literally pouring off my forehead. Soon we found ourselves being guided by a nurse through a long corridor with enormous, rather terrifying flowers with grotesque smiles on the wall.

'This used to be the children's wing,' the nurse explained.

'Not anymore?' I asked surprised. I had carefully calculated Bérénice's age the evening before. Even though I didn't remember the exact date of her birthday I was sure she must be five years old now.

'These days it's a wing for children and for adults,' said the nurse. She halted in front of one of the doors. Someone in there was shouting very loudly. The nurse indicated we should wait outside while she went in. She closed the door behind her, without locking it. Meneer Abdullah interpreted this as an invitation to gently push against the door and set it ajar. We saw how the nurse walked over to one of the patients, a man who had to be at least two metres tall.

The giant raised himself from his bed and turned with his back towards the nurse, offering her his hands. She tied them together behind his back. Next to me, I felt how Meneer Abdullah's breath stopped short. The shouting came from a man in the bed next to the chained giant. This man was entirely wrapped in a plaster cast. Only his face and his hands and feet were sticking out of the plaster. His swearing was loud and continuous.

Apart from the chained man and the man in plaster, there were four other patients in the room. A mistake on the nameplates attached to the beds first led us to sit down near the wrong bed – with an equally tragic expression on our faces. The nurse rectified our mistake, assuring us generously that it happened all the time. In all honesty, I hadn't recognized the child. She looked quite different from how I remembered. In my memory, she had braids. They had been cut off – rather unevenly as I would later find out. She was incredibly pale and incredibly thin, you could see the blue veins underneath her skin, especially near her forehead and on her arms. She wore a light blue pyjama jacket and brown trousers, nothing on her feet. She was lying down without moving, although her eyes were open. We sat down on two adjoining chairs next to Bérénice's bed.

'Dear Mother Maria,' I said. 'They've tied her up too.'

'She has beautiful, intelligent eyes,' said Meneer Abdullah.

An apple was lying on Bérénice's flat chest. She couldn't reach it though.

'Perhaps someone left it there but forgot to feed it to her,' I suggested. 'Perhaps it's because we came at the wrong time.'

At that moment another patient, a little boy, walked in, took the apple, urinated against the bed, made a rather obscene gesture quite unsuitable for his age, and ran off.

'I never thought I would say this,' said Meneer Abdullah, 'but your dog is much better trained than that boy.'

I wondered about the child. Her only reaction to us sitting next to her was to try and move away from us, but because of the chains she couldn't move away much. A social worker had told me something about an injury and about being a little behind compared to other children her age. How far behind exactly, I wondered, and in what way?

Meneer Abdullah reached out, wanting to touch the pale little hand closest to us with his own long dark fingers. The little hand immediately pulled back as much as the chains allowed. Meneer Abdullah drew his hand back too and used it to cover his mouth instead.

I tried to make out whether she resembled my brother or one of my parents. I didn't find any similarities but then I've never been very good at such things. I did see she was fortunate enough not to resemble me.

In school they used to say I look like a clown, ridiculous from afar but ugly as sin from nearby. My mother used to tell me otherwise but she ceased to fully convince me after the age of seven because once I was old enough to go to school I was also tall enough to look in the mirror and notice the repulsiveness of my big nose, my receding chin and my bushy clown's hair.

Bérénice's hair was light and thin. She had rather fine features and as far as I could tell, all the right proportions, and the right number of fingers and toes – thin as they were. On the whole she looked very, very small, everything about her being quite tiny except for her ears and her eyes (they made her look a little like a fairy on a mug once offered to me by an English colleague). She was crying, but without making any sound.

'I say we untie her and run really fast,' said Meneer Abdullah, after looking over his shoulder to make sure no nurses were listening in.

'I'm not sure if she's able to walk,' I answered and pointed at the left leg, which was in plaster.

'We'll carry her,' suggested Meneer Abdullah, 'and then we'll…'

It was somewhat difficult to talk because the man in plaster's swearing was so loud. He was wrestling with his plaster cast and vomiting up a stream of very politically incorrect curses, directed especially at Meneer Abdullah.

Meneer Abdullah got up from his chair and started walking over to the swearing man.

'Where are you going?' I asked in dismay.

'Don't worry, I know what I'm doing,' said Meneer Abdullah. 'All that man wants is a little bit of attention. That's what everybody wants in the end. Trust me.'

He walked towards the bed with the swearing man and held out his hand. The man shut up for a moment, probably as surprised as I was, and Meneer Abdullah shook his hand.

'Good afternoon, Sir, very pleased to meet you. Abdalrahman Abdullah, at your service! With whom have I the honour?'

The man pulled Meneer Abdullah's hand, lifted himself off the bed and let himself and his heavy cast fall on top of the unwanted visitor. Then he tried to bite Meneer Abdullah's ear. Meneer Abdullah let out a small cry. I ran over and tried to pull the man off Meneer Abdullah. At this point, the very tall man in the adjoining bed let out a loud roar, broke his chains and jumped on top of me, entangling his fingers in my grey locks.

It took a whole team of big male nurses and a large syringe to unravel us all.

'It's been a long time since he saw such a lovely head of hair,' said one of the male nurses about the tall man who was still clenching a couple of grey wisps in his hands and had now started biting his wrists. 'In here, we cut off everything.'

'I totally understand,' I said, rubbing my new bald spots.

'Léopold managed to get loose again,' said the male nurse to another male nurse who had just come in with an extra syringe.

'What set him off this time?' asked the other male nurse. 'Was it female hair again?'

'Yeah, afraid so. Oh I'm sorry sir, I didn't mean it that way. It's just that Léopold really gets quite excited by long hair. He's always had it. Used to drive his mum crazy, poor thing.'

'My hair's not that long,' I said.

'Yeah, he did have quite a nasty go at you there, sir.'

'I've never had it cut too short either. My mother used to think it quite becoming,' I confessed.

'I'm sure it was, sir.'

'She always thought it made me look a little like an absent minded professor. She was very proud to have a son going to university. I am a professor, by the way. Professor Jean-Claude van Bouillon.'

'I'm sorry I didn't realize before. Are you alright now, Professor?'

'I'm not sure. I seem to have lost my handkerchief.'

I was still sitting on the floor, leaning against one of the beds, like Meneer Abdullah. The male nurse gave me a little flannel to wipe the sweat off my face, while the other male nurses crouched on the floor too, trying to re-gain control of the tall man who had attacked me.

'Who tied him up? We really need stronger chains.'

'It's a disgrace,' said Meneer Abdullah. 'A total disgrace.'

'I'm very sorry about what happened to you, sir, are you bruised very badly?'

'I'm not talking about those few insignificant scratches, my good man,' said Meneer Abdullah while trying to dam a stream of blood on his forehead with my third handkerchief. 'I'm talking about the disgrace of keeping people chained up like that, like animals. No wonder they go half mad. No wonder they start attacking innocent passers-by. No wonder this country is in the miserable state it is. It is a total disgrace and that's all I have to say about it. To chain up perfectly healthy, innocent young men who are in the prime of their life!'

The man in the plaster cast let out a loud roar and resumed another long tirade of very politically incorrect curses, again primarily aimed at Meneer Abdullah.

'Keeping him in plaster is the only way to keep him at all, sir,' said the nurse. 'If you have a better idea we'd be interested to hear it but believe me, we have tried everything we could think of.'

'Surely there must be something you can do! Anything that doesn't involve chaining people up!'

'There is only one hospital in the country where they are equipped to deal with this sort of thing,' said the nurse, 'but they have a very limited availability of beds. All the other patients end up in psychiatric institutions, like this one.'

I pulled Meneer Abdullah's arm before he could continue discussing.

'We have to look at the child,' I said, reminding him of why we had come there. 'I am going to try and adopt her.'

Poems

John White

A Case

One evening we retrieved it
redding out the attic – oxblood
under a pillar of clouds,
saw spilling out his diagnostic kit
syringes, scalpel, spatula
as if from a conjurer's hat.

A kitchen pops up. Sewing together
the split head of some half-tight critter
toppled from his bike, no anaesthetic
needed, there's a tap: the milkman envoy
torn between the priest and doctor
only serves to keep the wound green.
Nights he'd open out on a russet moor
to catch a man of that ward turned lunatic
by tongue-subduing shadows.

Well he knew the terror
in a smir of rain – the caked boots
spinning a good yard above
the floor; how thinking made it so –
the lone farm house where peak
succeeds to trough that even in a deluge

was bridgeable.
                    Clicking it shut
we lugged it back there with its grain and heft
and felt the dust rising, the wind whistling through.

Also like him

The slow tramp to the kirk, the laying down
is done now. Folk drift down October lanes.
The Book says *man goeth to his long home* –
a dark-eyed house with heavy-lidded panes.
That spirit-quickening psalm of yesterday
ignited even my raw stuttering breath;
now clacking crows cloaked in a parody
of mourning fill the expanding emptiness.
This 'emptiness', the door shut to the street,
is habit-forming, soon solidifies,
or so I reckon, raking leaves, back straight
and (also like him) smiling with widening eyes.
Next door an engine revs up – labour of love.
A boy is playing 'Chopsticks' up above.

Tullanee

I swung the rented motor grass-wards out
of harm's way pondering how the name
they'd christened it in ancient days still suited
the old place, *hill of the raven*,
that snarl of wind and twigs and blackened roots.

They fed the vexed Elijah bread and meat,
this lumpen crowd of outsize choughs
each squat and plumed in Calvinistic gown
above that barn now dignified to *chorch*,
the thorn that's left after the rose has gone.

The skyline's sometimes haze, more often mist.
Today the creeping Foyle's so distant
it's congealed, like you could walk to Inishowen
 and back, drop in to catch a singsong
in Moville and hardly wet your feet.

Midway up the slope the weather turns.
Rain runs across my back burning like ice
from off the trees and onto headstones
(*Let not your heart be troubled* my father's text)
 forever overlooking and overlooked.

It stops and all you catch is the still small voice
of a dripping tap on hand for you to water
flowers either clouding under glass
like breathing eyes or wetter than a trifle
beneath branches stiff as tuning forks

that once had stoked the stumbling faithful,
one of whom nods back to me - it's better left
unsaid, this slippery path, the whispering air
about our heads, birds fidgeting in nests
become enormous year by year.

Apples

I

One who knew was Uncle Tom
who'd show you how to cup
the apple, twist the stem.

He came from Portadown
the orchard country, took up
with my aunt who'd have thrown

a peel over her shoulder
unbroken, or lodged the pips
discreetly in the fire

and saw they fitted to a T.
In North Tyrone he'd switch
to other produce, slowly.

Tomatoes were his pride,
the apple's life from stalk
to flower unsafe – a fusillade

would fall and sweetly seep
into the soil, slug black
fit only for the cider heap,

not sturdy like the apple
crops of old. At home I climb
a ladder so unstable

I've my mother deaved
with worry, freckled limbs
stretched out in firm belief

I'm fit to reach the stars.
The gods eat apples and stay young
the pagans said. My ladder's

heading for a fall.
I cup my knee, stunned,
branded brown and purple.

II

We're talking planters
rather than the wild, the 'bitter
apple' only a young elephant
could eat but which with soap
a rarity would nicely lather up
when sliced and rubbed,
or the 'Sodom' - once reputed
to dissolve in ash and smoke
if plucked, but on parched plains
quenches the Grants and 'Tommies':
what gazelles have found to work
the tribesmen ape, boiling the roots
to fortify their stomachs.

III

For my sister

All that training just to paint
domestic scenes – my mother's cookers
hanging green beside the hedge,
the whitewashed wall behind
of the Orange Hall where once Big Ian
had stood on top of a trailer in a strop
and swore he'd drive the Southern foe
into the sea and hold them under
with such sturdy lungs we had no need
to prise open the bedroom window.

John White

Pity on the Gourd

(*Jonah 4: 10 - 11*)

Ambidextrous, I was scorned like Nineveh.
Not that I mixed up right and left
but rather took to switching hands whenever
I had reached midway, would barely lift

the pen from off the page. Teachers believed
me idle, drifting: 'He'll have to settle
on the one hand'. With the time I'd left
I peered out windows, dozed off counting cattle.

Symposium

'So tell us,' someone asks 'about Limavady".*
'...Jumped this gorge,' big Dessie drawls 'to fetch
a written warning, just too late for Chiefs
who got all sequestered for a cabbage patch'.

*

Cross-country was a sharp left out
the hind gate panting towards O'Cahan's Rock
where due west Mullagh Hill lay, and Drumceatt.
Our parties stopped off at the first grassy poke.

Spring rolled into summer, French to Shakespeare.
Then there were giants. The same master ran
Biology and Scripture Union: a legend.
A blind harpist stumbled on his *derriere*.

We gathered seeking revelation – girls
emerged in hockey shirts and the iron
Roe curled round the edge of town
and the bombed station from the holy well.

*

'The message was in the mouth' declared
our swami. Hard by rain-drenched fields
were sweating ornaments in green and gold.
'That's one account. You always have the collar.'

* *Limavady* (Irish) – the leap of the dog

Beyond Gosoba

Dancing barefoot around the special school
draws glances like a monkey god.
A lightness gathers with each footfall,
ball games brush with riot by a blade
of grass, here in this *al fresco* call-centre
in which all ground is hallowed.

And so one day as tar churns into butter
we lurch faltering on a seaward slope
beyond the Hamilton house that bothers
me, a dream turned midden or a coop
for hens where books are being hawked
like flypaper. By now we've given up

on know-how. Back on board our sloop this rake
(our guide) spells out the woes of honey catchers
stood astride a skein of oil and fish-hooks.
Downstream mangrove roots manoeuvre
crab-like upwards. Slow, with head of pin
the water monitor is monitored.

And the only sign of tiger is of prints
in sand (a bored day-tripper spills
his *Cobra*) but I'm reeling at the orphan
magnitude of holes, great shovels full
borne hither. Like a first cutting of hair
or horoscope cast. Birthday. Something awful.

1973

Gerard Woodward

1973

(Extract from a novel)

The viewing area designated by the Port Authorities was the crumbling, ivy-tangled graveyard of Topnot village church, on the opposite side of the river.

'I used to come here as a little girl,' said Toby's mother, 'for Sunday school. We lived in Topnot for a few years when I was younger.'

They were walking briskly along, Toby in a little brown suit borrowed from somewhere, his mother in a rather stiff woollen dress, having taken the train from Leastways, over the Lion to Shanks, and from there along the Isle Of Arther road to Topnot, a walk of about a quarter of a mile. Toby was tired, and was having trouble keeping up with his mother's great clumping strides.

Topnot church was a sulky, flinty little structure built close to the river bank, its graveyard wall being the dead's last defence against the slimy tidal reach of the Lion, whose herring-stench was particularly strong here.

'Where is everyone?' Toby's mother said, when they arrived in the empty churchyard, 'I thought there would be hundreds of people here.' But there were only the graves, each with its gracefully carved tombstone, on many of which the word 'drowned' was prominent. Toby regarded the place as a playground, and began climbing on table-top tombs, and running in and out of the graves, now and then stopping to read one.

'Mum, what does 'deceased' mean?'

'I can't believe it,' said his mother, approaching the graveyard wall and looking out across the river, 'Someone has played the most awful joke on me. Look, everyone's over there.'

Toby ran over to join his mother, and started climbing up on the graveyard wall, before stopping to take in the magnificence of the view. Across a stretch of perhaps a thousand yards of water, some muddy channels and little reedy islands, the largest of which had a low circular fort on it (a defence against Napoleon's navy), were the pitched roofs and lofty cranes of Lionbridge Dockyards with, at the centre, like the giant Gulliver attended by Lilliputians, the vast white structure of RMS Lionbridge, the second biggest cruise liner ever built, fifty thousand tons, nine hundred feet from bow to stern. She seemed like a gargantuan pearl shining in a universe of mud and slime. Side on to the river, her entire profile was resplendently on display, the exquisitely sharp lines of her bows making her seem beaked, like a heron. Her funnels, streamlined and angled backwards like the fletching on an arrow, added to the impression that she was designed for speed. Her bridge was sleekly curved and glazed with tinted glass. Such delicacy of line could make one forget her size – cabin portholes in rows up her sides like skyscraper windows, decks stacked on top of each other like the layers of a wedding cake – it hardly seemed believable that such a thing could ever move, let alone float on water.

'That's a big boat,' said Toby, a note of accusation in his voice, as though it was fundamentally unfair for a boat to be that big.

'It *is* a big boat, Toby, the biggest boat ever built by Lionbridge Dockyards, and maybe the last, who knows?'

'Is that the boat Daddy built?'

'Yes, Toby, Daddy helped build that boat.'

'Is that where Daddy died?'

'Yes Toby.'

'How did he die?'

'Well, you know Toby. I've told you many times. Daddy had a very nasty accident in the dockyards when he was building RMS Lionbridge.'

'Why?'

'Why? Well, people have accidents all the time.'

'How did he die?'

Toby was asking these questions casually, as if he couldn't have cared less about the answers. But his mother did her best to provide them.

'Well, you see those cranes? One of those cranes was dangling a great big chain onto the ground, and Daddy's foot got caught in one of the links. Then the crane did this funny thing that is called a whiplash, which only happens when the winding gear seizes up, but it meant that Daddy was pulled up into the air by his foot.'

'And did that make him die?'

'Not in itself, although it wasn't very pleasant, and I'm sure lots of people were trying to save him, but he was dangling upside down and the crane was out of control and they were probably shouting Help! Help! Mr Lott's foot's caught in the chain! And I dare say he was swinging about upside down over the half-built RMS Lionbridge shouting Get me down! Get me down! And going red like you do when you're upside down, and it must have been funny for him because the river must have been in the sky and the sky must have been in the ground... Well, how high do you think those cranes are? They're two hundred feet high when they're stretched right up, and your poor old Daddy was pulled all the way up to the top, and do you see what there is at the top of the chain (although they use cables now, thank goodness, and not chains), what can you see, right at the end of the crane's arm?'

'A wheel,' said Toby, squinting.

'That's right, it's a great big metal wheel that runs the chain through the jib. Well I bet the man driving the crane was pulling all the levers he could find because he didn't want Daddy to get pulled over the wheel, because if he'd got pulled over the wheel he'd have been squashed just like a lemon in a sock going through a mangle. But unfortunately, the driver couldn't stop Daddy going up and up and up, and that's what happened to him, he went straight through the wheel – pop. And you know, Toby, Daddy's blood must have showered the half built carcass of RMS Lionbridge which lay below him. So now we can look at that great ship and think Daddy, a part of you lives on in RMS Lionbridge. That's your true memorial in this world.'

'That's a nice story,' said Toby, looking carefully and affectionately at the ship.

There was a great deal of activity on the water. Every boat was out on the river. There were two grey destroyers and an aircraft carrier downstream, pilot ships with their tall funnels and low bodies patrolling further upstream. There was the paddle steamer, SS Ghuznee Fort, which was laden to sinking point with passengers. Indeed, the Napoleonic fort on the island was also full of people, there was even a brass band out there, whose parpings were rather drowned out by the greater noises of the reach.

'That's not fair, look,' said Toby's mother, 'people have been allowed on the island. I've never been allowed on the island in all my life. We could have gone there today, Toby. You could have been a little sailor after all, just like your dear Daddy wanted you to be.'

Earlier that morning, getting dressed in their Sunday best clothes for the launch of RMS Lionbridge, adjusting his tie for him, his mother had said to Toby

'And have you decided what you want to be when you grow up, Toby?'

'Yes mummy.'

'Oh goody. And so what are you going to be?'

'A zookeeper.'

His mother didn't smile as he'd expected her to. Instead she looked serious and troubled.

'I'm afraid that's where you are wrong little Toby. You see, the truth is that you are going to be a sailor. Haven't I always told you that?'

'But I like zebras.'

'Listen Toby. If you became a sailor you could sail anywhere in the world and see all the zebras you wanted. And penguins, polar bears. Let's have no more talk of zoo-keeping,' she briefly strangled Toby as she tightened his tie for him, 'and let us talk instead about the life of a sailor. It is a grand life…'

It was a life Toby was to hear a great deal about over the years. She would tell him stories about his grandfather, who was a sailor, and his great great grandfather before him, who was captain of The Gorgon, (or was it The Hector?), how he had been a prisoner on Martinique, how he had been a castaway on Norfolk Island, how he captured twenty ships in a six month tour of duty. Toby liked hearing these stories. They gave him a sense of a firm foundation for his existence. He might lack a father, but he still had a history, and a powerful one, full of adventures and colourful characters. But he still didn't want to be a sailor.

'Why didn't Daddy become a sailor?'

But Toby's mother was done with talking about her husband. She was giving her full attention to the spectacle before her, the teeming waters of the Lion, and the towering white monolith that was RMS Lionbridge, the ship that would carry the city's name around the world for decades to come.

'She's a magnificent beast,' said Toby's mother. 'Do you know, Toby, there isn't another ship of that size in the world that that sort of hull? A revolutionary design. A planing hull that behaves like a displacement hull, like you get on yacht, with a flat keel. That thing could handle like a speedboat, and you'd get hardly any roll. No one would ever get seasick on RMS Lionbridge. That's why they are launching her sideways, to demonstrate her stability and buoyancy in the most effective way. This is all passing over your little head, isn't it, Toby? You're wondering how your old Ma can know so much about boats when she hasn't stepped off dry land since the day she was born. Put it down to a boyhood fascination with boats.'

'Boyhood?'

'Yes, I mean your father was absolutely silly about boats when he was a boy. Used to bore the knickers off me, with his model boats. Listen to that sound, they've started up the horns.'

A tremendous echoey wail had gone up, like the dying calls of a school of sea monsters, as every ship that was currently on the river, and there must have been twenty or more, sounded their foghorns together, continuously. The city of Lionbridge was putting everything it had into this launch.

With the launch of the ship the dockyard faced an uncertain future. There had already been layoffs. A small amount of work repairing royal navy frigates had been made available, and some investment had been made into converting a dock for submarine repair, but otherwise prospects were bleak. Rumours abounded that the launch of RMS Lionbridge would be sabotaged, the slipway tampered with, so that ship would be forever remain on dry land. But now it seemed that the moment had come, the festoons of balloons and streamers were waving, the brass bands were thumping through their limited repertoires, the sirens were wailing up and down the reach, and, just visible to Toby and his mother, the crowds that had gathered close to the ship itself were cheering.

'Look', said Toby's mother, 'they've let them in right up to the propellers, they're practically crawling over her.'

And, all alone on the far shore of the river, Toby and his mother watched as if from another country, the weird customs and tribal rituals of an island continent.

'Lord, it's moving,' said Toby's mother, clutching her son with a sudden steely grip, as though afraid of losing him, 'it's moving, Toby, oh God, I can't believe it...'

Imperceptibly at first, the great white beast began to slide towards the waters of the Lion.

'Too fast, Toby, look, it's leaning, Oh the saints...'

Something had gone wrong. One of the carriages had buckled, perhaps through sabotage, more likely because they were wrongly stressed, which meant that RMS Lionbridge rolled down the slipway at an angle far more acute than intended. Having never seen a ship launched sideways at the Lionbridge Dockyards, few people recognized that anything was wrong, not until the wave came. As she hit the water, a great white wave unfolded itself and rippled out in all directions. The first to feel its force were those standing on a small jetty about a hundred yards upstream of the slipway, they must have watched in horror as the wave oozed towards them along the bank, like a tidal bore, scattering those who were close to the shoreline. Then, when it met the wooden jetty, it swept straight through and over it, flinging the crowds into the river. The Lionbridge Chronicle later reported that eighty-seven people had been swept into the river Lion from this jetty, but only one of those had drowned. In the other direction, downstream, the bore-like wave swept down the bank without causing any damage. As the wave spread out into the river, those boats nearby began to lurch and sway as the wave hit them, and Toby fancied that he could hear the cries of anguish from those gathered on the fort island, as they saw the wave approach them. This low-lying marshy strip had no defences whatsoever against a wave of that size. The parping of the tubas stopped as the musicians and all others on the island dashed for the shelter of the fort itself. Were those flickering glints of gold and silver really trumpets and trombones horns being scattered into the air as the musicians ran for it? But most of them had made their move too late. The wave swept across the island like a waitress lazily clearing a table, the musicians, the gathered families, the aunts and uncles and all the children were washed away into the waters of the Lion. Around a hundred and seventy people were cast into the river from this island, the paper later reported, but none were drowned or even seriously injured. The paper called this fact a 'miracle'.

Now it was only Toby and his mother who were left in the path of the wave, but it had lost a great deal of its energy by the time it reached the wall of Topnot Graveyard. They watched its approach with curiosity rather than fear. The wave was now only about three feet high, which meant it slopped against the graveyard wall and sent up a sheet of dark brown salty water that showered Toby and his mother. Toby laughed. Looking out across the river they could see many people struggling in the water, flailing arms and splashing legs, and much screaming and wailing. No one on earth now seemed to notice the magnificent ship, stabilized on the waters of the Lion, clouds of helium-filled balloons drifting up into the sky from its decks. It might as well have not been there.

Biographical Notes

Paula Bardowell Stanic has an MSt in Creative Writing from Oxford University. Her play *What's Lost* won the 2008 Alfred Fagon Award. *Late Night Shopping*, a short, was part of 'The Outsiders' season (White Bear Theatre) and was published in *Brand*, and *The Packingtown Review*, Chicago. *6 Minutes* was part of Soho Theatre's rapid response to the recession season *Everything Must Go*. Her play *Monday* for Red Ladder Theatre Company was short-listed for the 2009 John Whiting Award.

Elleke Boehmer has published four novels, including *Screens against the Sky* (short-listed for the David Higham Prize, 1990), *Bloodlines* (short-listed for the Sanlam Prize, 2000), and *Nile Baby* (2008). Her first volume of short stories, *Sharmilla, and Other Portraits*, came out in summer 2010. She is Professor of World Literatures in English at the University of Oxford and has published, amongst other academic books, *Stories of Women* (2005).

Mark Burton is an Oxfordshire-born writer who has worked on such comedy stalwarts as *Spitting Image*, *Alas Smith & Jones*, and *Have I Got News For You*. He went on to co-write the animation films *Madagascar*, and *Wallace & Gromit: Curse of the Wererabbit*, as well as the children's film *Aliens In the Attic* for Twentieth Century Fox.

Manish Chauhan is a British-Indian writer whose themes include family relationships and sexual identity. He has written many short stories and is currently working on his first novel, *The Bloomers*, which is set in his birth place, Leicester. He is a graduate of Oxford's MSt in Creative Writing.

Stephanie Chong gave up her job as a commercial litigator at a Canadian law firm to pursue her passion for fiction. In March 2009, she received her PhD in Comparative Literature from the University of Toronto and six months later completed her MSt in Creative Writing at Oxford University, gaining a Distinction.

David Constantine's most recent volume of poetry is *Nine Fathom Deep* (Bloodaxe 2009). With his wife Helen he edits *Modern Poetry in Translation*.

Fred D'Aguiar's fifth novel is *Bethany Bettany* (Vintage, 2003). His sixth poetry collection, *Continental Shelf* (Carcanet, 2009), was a Poetry Book Society Summer Choice and shortlisted for the TS Eliot Prize 2009. He teaches at Virginia Tech.

Sarah Darby was long-listed for the Bridport Poetry prize and has had poetry published in journals and an anthology. Her short fiction won an award supported by the British Heart Foundation. She works within the NHS, using writing to help patients with long-term conditions.

Roy Davids was Head of the Department of Books and Manuscripts at Sotheby's for many years and additionally Marketing Director for five. He ran his own business as a manuscript dealer from 1994 to 2006. He is author of *White Noise*, 2006, a pamphlet of poems produced by the Acumen Press, and is presently compiling a book on provenance in Chinese ceramics.

Greg Delanty's latest book is *Collected Poems, 1986-2006* (Carcanet Press, 2006). He has received many awards, most recently a Guggenheim for poetry. He teaches at Saint Michael's College Vermont, and returns to his home in Ireland for part of the year. He is presently the Vice President of the Association of Literary Scholars and Critics and will be President this coming year.

Jane Draycott is a 'Next Generation' poet (Arts Council/Poetry Book Society 2004), who has been nominated three times for the Forward Prize for Poetry. Her latest collection *'Over'* was shortlisted for the 2009 T. S. Eliot prize. In 2008 she was a Stephen Spender prizewinner for an extract from her new translation of the medieval dream-vision 'Pearl', due from Carcanet/OxfordPoets in 2011.

Frank Egerton studied English at Keble College, Oxford, and has reviewed fiction for *The Times*, *TLS* and *Financial Times*. He is interested in both the close examination of fiction and how recent technologies are changing the publishing industry. His first novel, *The Lock*, was published in 2003 and his second, *Invisible*, was reissued by StreetBooks in October 2010.

Jonathan Evans has written over sixty commissioned scripts for a number of popular TV series. His feature film script, *Act Your Age,* is in development with the UK Film Council, and he has recently completed an animation feature script for Neomis Animation, Paris. Jonathan has worked as a television storyliner for Pearson Television, Grundy International and Hewson International and has assessed movie scripts for Buena Vista.

Jane Griffiths was born in Exeter, but brought up in Holland. She read English at Oxford, and returned there (after a period working as a bookbinder and lexicographer) for a doctorate on the Tudor poet John Skelton. She has lectured at Oxford and Edinburgh, and is now at the University of Bristol. Her latest book, *Another Country* (Bloodaxe, 2008) was shortlisted for the Forward Award for Best Collection.

Sabyn Javeri-Jillani was born in Pakistan and lives in London. Her short stories have been published in *The London Magazine*, *Wasafiri*, *SHE*, *Trespass*, *World Audience* and as the title story in the anthologies *And the World Changed* (Feminist Press NY) and in *Neither Night Nor Day* (Harper Collins). She is a graduate of Oxford University's MSt in Creative Writing.

Christina Koning has worked as a travel writer and journalist – most recently for the *Times*. Her novels include *A Mild Suicide*, which was short-listed for the David Higham Prize for Fiction; *Undiscovered Country*, which won the Encore Prize and was long-listed for the Orange Prize, and *Fabulous Time*, which was awarded a Society of Authors Travelling Scholarship. Her latest novel is *The Dark Tower* (2010).

David Krump received the Florence Khan Memorial Award, the Ruth Lilly Poetry Fellowship, the Lorine Niedecker Award, the Poetry Foundation/ Newberry Library Fellowship in American Poetry, and the 2009 Dorothy Sargent Rosenberg Prize for 'young poets of unusual promise.' His first play, *5,000 Pounds,* earned him a nomination for the 2010 Princess Grace Award for Playwriting. He teaches at Viterbo University and serves as poetry editor for *Poets & Artists*.

Grevel Lindop lives in Manchester, where he was a Professor of English at the University until 2001. He has published six books of poems with Carcanet Press, including *Selected Poems* (2001) and *Playing With Fire* (2006). His *A Literary Guide to the Lake District* (1993) won the Lakeland Book of the Year Award and *Travels on the Dance Floor* was a BBC Radio 4 Book of the Week in 2008 and shortlisted for Authors' Club Best Travel Book.

Nicholas McInerny is a screenwriter and dramatist with over 75 credits in film, television, stage and radio. He was Creative Arts Fellow at Wolfson College, Oxford and is currently Chair of Script, the West Midlands Agency for Dramatic Writers.

Deborah Mason teaches English to international students at Oxford University Language Centre, where she is the Assistant Director. She has been writing poetry since 2000, and has had poems published in a wide variety of journals over the last decade. She is a member of Kellogg College and the Back Room Poets.

Will May is an Oxford-based poet and composer. He has set poems by Sylvia Plath and B.S. Johnson, and his work has been performed on BBC Radio 3. In 2004 he was awarded the Lord Alfred Douglas Memorial Prize. He is a currently a Research Fellow at the University of Southampton, where he is working on a project looking at collaborations between British poets and composers.

Clare Morgan is Director of Oxford University's MSt in Creative Writing, a member of the English Faculty, and a Fellow of Kellogg College. Her publications include a collection of stories, *An Affair of the Heart*, and *What Poetry Brings to Business*, (University of Michigan Press 2010). Her new novel, *A Book for All and None*, is forthcoming with Weidenfeld and Nicolson in April 2011. She reviews regularly for the *Times Literary Supplement*.

Lucy Newlyn is Professor of English Language and Literature, and Fellow in English at St Edmund Hall, Oxford. She has published widely on English Romantic literature, and is an authority on Wordsworth and Coleridge. Currently she is working on the prose of Edward Thomas for OUP. With Guy Cuthbertson, she published *Branch-Lines: Edward Thomas and Contemporary Poetry* with Enitharmon. Her first collection of poems *Ginnel* was published by Oxford*Poets*/Carcanet in 2005.

Colm O'Shea has a PhD in English Literature and an MSt in Creative Writing from Oxford University. He has read for London and New York screenplay agencies, and published articles on film and philosophy, including for *Bright Lights*. His poetry was anthologised in *Voice Recognition: 21 Poets for the 21st Century* (Bloodaxe, 2009), *Poets from Britain and America: a White Leaf Anthology* (2009), and *Sentence: Journal of Prose Poetics* (2010). He teaches expository writing at NYU.

Annette Pas, born to a Dutch father and a Flemish mother, grew up in Bruges and later moved to England. She graduated from Oxford University's MSt in Creative Writing, and is currently writing up her PhD in Psychology. She has been involved with the reorganization of Child Protection and Children's Services in the UK, and has written about education, culture and dialogue. She speaks four languages.

Tim Pears was born in Kent, brought up in Devon and has lived in Montgomeryshire and Oxford. He writes novels, short stories and essays on sport. His sixth novel, *Landed* (William Heinemann) was published in March 2010.

Aaron Rench is a literary agent and a graduate of Oxford University with an MSt in Creative Writing. Since founding Leaptide Literary Group he has also begun producing films, including the feature documentary, *Collision*. His poetry most recently appeared in the *Oxford Magazine*. He and his wife live in the US with their three children.

Rita Ricketts is currently a Bodleian Visiting Scholar undertaking research at Merton College, and has hosted writers' events in New Zealand and the UK. Researching for her book *Adventurers All*, she found common cause with the Blackwells who made their publishing debut launching writers 'unknown to fame'. From this historical base grew the *World Writers at Blackwell* series, On the Fringe at Sunday Times Oxford Literary Festival and now *Initiate*.

Sophy Roberts is a journalist based in West Dorset. She writes regularly on culture and travel for *The Financial Times* and the US edition of *Departures* magazine, for which she is Editor-at-Large. Her novel-in-progress *The Butterfly Tide* won the 2009 A. M. Heath prize for fiction, dedicated to graduates of Oxford's MSt in Creative Writing.

David Shook attended graduate school at Oxford, finishing with distinction. His work has appeared or is forthcoming in Ambit, Agenda, Oxford Magazine, Poetry, Poetry London, Wasafiri, World Literature Today, and elsewhere. His chapbook of translations of Zapotec poet Víctor Terán is available from the Poetry Translation Centre, and a selection of his own poems appears in OxfordPoets 2010 (Carcanet). Shook lives in Los Angeles, where he edits Molossus.

Sudeep Sen studied at Delhi and Columbia, and was a visiting scholar at Harvard University. His books include: *Postmarked India: New & Selected Poems* (HarperCollins), *Rain, Aria (AK Ramanujan Translation Award)*, *Letters of Glass* and *The HarperCollins Book of English Poetry by Indians* (editor). *Blue Nude: Poems & Translations 1977-2012 (Jorge Zalamea International Poetry Award)* is forthcoming. He is the editorial director of Aark Arts and editor of *Atlas*. [www.atlasaarkarts.net]

Rose Solari is the author of two full-length collections of poetry, *Orpheus in the Park* and *Difficult Weather*. Her poetry has appeared in many anthologies, including *American Poetry: The Next Generation* (Carnegie Mellon University Press). Her awards include the Randall Jarrell Poetry Prize, an Academy of American Poets University Prize, and numerous grants. She was Blackwell Books Poet-in-Residence for the 2009 Sunday Times Literary Fringe Festival in Oxford.

Jesselynn Sutanto is a graduate of the Universities of Oxford and California, Berkeley. She is currently residing in Oxford, where she continues to write about the misadventures of Delima.

Zoe Teale read English at Oxford University and Social Anthropology at the London School of Economics. Her first novel, *Sir Phoebus's Ma*, was published by Orion in 1995. She is currently Chair of the Trustees of The Allen Lane Foundation which was set up by the founder of Penguin Books, her grandfather Sir Allen Lane. She lives in Oxford and has two children.

Tonnie Walls is an American writer. His poems have appeared in *Oxford Magazine*, *Markings*, *Aesthetica*, and *Poetica Magazine*. Translations were also published in Bulgarian daily, *Trud*. Tonnie, a graduate of Oxford University's MSt in Creative Writing, is now working on his second novel.

John White was born in County Londonderry. He has been published in various magazines as well as the Carcanet anthology Oxford Poets 2007. After completing a Masters in Creative Writing at Oxford University, he recently took a year out to do voluntary work in schools in Africa and India. He is now back living and working in Oxfordshire. 'Also Like Him' first appeared in *Oxford Magazine* and *Oxford Poets 2007* (Carcanet). 'Tullanee' and 'Apples' first appeared in *Agenda* magazine.

Alice Willington was born in Scotland and now lives in Oxford. She has recently completed the MSt in Creative Writing at Oxford University. Her first publication was her poem 'Cartography', which was published in *Avocado Magazine*. She has subsequently had poems published in the on-line literary journals *Horizon Review*, *Molossus*, and *New Linear Perspectives* She was shortlisted for the Bridport Prize in 2008 and was awarded second prize in the 2009 Ledbury Poetry Competition. She currently works for the University of Oxford Development Office.

Gerard Woodward has published four poetry collections, the first of which, *Householder* (1991), won a Somerset Maugham Award. His first novel, *August*, was shortlisted for the 2001 Whitbread First Novel Award, and was followed in 2004 by *I'll Go To Bed At Noon*, shortlisted for the Man Booker Prize, and *A Curious Earth* (2007). He is Professor of Creative Writing at Bath Spa University and his most recent publication is a collection of stories, *Caravan Thieves* (2008).

Roy Woolley was born in Derby and studied at the universities of Kent, Liverpool, London and Manchester before completing the MSt in Creative Writing at Oxford University, specialising in Poetry. His work has appeared in *The Wolf*, *Poetry News*, *The Harvard Gay and Lesbian Review*, and on the poetry blog *Peony Moon*. He was one of the winners in the 2010 Oxford Parallel UniVerse poetry competition.

For further information, or to contact the contributors please email:
college.office@kellogg.ox.ac.uk or telephone: +44 (0)1865 612000.

Please note that no unsolicited submission are accepted.

Acknowledgements

The President of Kellogg College, Professor Jonathan Michie, and the Fellows, especially Angus Hawkins, Jitka Fort, Michael Yudkin, Chris Davies, Anna Beer, Cathy Oakes and other friends and colleagues among the Fellowship who have supported the initiation and production of this anthology through the Kellogg College Centre for Creative Writing. Especial thanks to Rebecca Rue for her invaluable administrative and logistical input, and to Ana Pastega for her generous support; to Enge Marshall for his help in proofreading; and to the whole Blackwell production team for their tremendous contribution. The anthology would not have come to fruition without the tireless dedication of the editorial panel – Jane Draycott, Frank Egerton and Jon Evans – and we are very grateful to them, and to whose writers already experienced in the world of publication who have contributed to this anthology with such enthusiasm and thereby demonstrated their belief in our aims.

The President of Blackwell's, Julian Blackwell, for his enduring support; The Warden (Dame Professor Jessica Rawson) and Fellows of Merton, especially Julia Walworth, Simon Jones and archivist Julian Reid; Bodley's Librarian Sarah Thomas, Richard Ovenden and senior colleagues: Clive Hurst and Chris Fletcher; Philip Carpenter of Wiley Blackwell; Christopher Ricks, Jon Stallworthy, Bernard O'Donoghue, Greg Delanty; Oxford Poetry especially Carmen Bugan and others 'known to fame' who led sessions and encouraged new writers; Sally Dunsmore, Director of the Sunday Times Literary Festival and Tim Eustace who first gave us hope that the Blackwell Board would be receptive to a publication.

Copyright Holders